THE LAKE DISTRICT AND CUMBRIA

D. M. Clifton

CONTENTS

Published by Collins
Glasgow and London
First Published 1976

Cover photograph of Rydal Water is reproduced by permission of John Woolverton

Maps by John McWilliam

Drawings by Ian Harley

*Photographs by courtesy of
Peter Baker (title page, pages 42 bottom, 55, 65)
British Tourist Authority (page 17 top and bottom)
J. Allan Cash (pages 8, 13, 22, 25, 27, 28–9, 33, 39, 42 top, 52, 60, 69 top and bottom)*

ISBN 0 00 435744 2

THE LAKE DISTRICT AND CUMBRIA

INTRODUCING LAKELAND

Lakeland is different. Nowhere else in England did the great glaciers of the Ice Age produce such spectacular formations of mountain and lake, likened in many ways to the Alps. Rugged, craggy peaks of the mountain ranges form a magnificent backcloth in every direction. Heather and bracken-covered lower fells enfold and are reflected in the still waters of the many lakes and tarns with which the area abounds. A purple haze on distant fells is interspersed by rocky outcrops and interlaced with lines of silver, where ghylls (mountain streams) tumble into the valley. Ancient villages and small dale chapels, whose beauty lies in the stark simplicity of their interiors, perpetuate the peaceful atmosphere so beloved of William Wordsworth and John Ruskin. The isolation of hill farmers, who rely on their black and white collies to round up the flocks of sure-footed sheep over the rough terrain, contrasts strongly with the hustle of the lakeside holiday resorts, where the beauty of the lakes in their sylvan surroundings can be appreciated to the full from the water. Facilities for watersports and other pastimes are provided on Coniston, Windermere, Grasmere, Derwent Water and Ullswater; climbers will equally appreciate the opportunity to scale England's highest mountains. Outdoor activities in the summer are limitless, and visitors may enjoy traditional Lakeland sports including the Ambleside and Grasmere Games, hound trailing, fell racing and Cumberland wrestling.

Millions of people come to Lakeland each year, and it is hoped that this book, which has been divided into three sections for easy reference, will help to explain some of the reasons for its immense popularity. The first section deals with history, customs, travel facilities, activity holidays and the types of accommodation available. The second section gives suggested touring routes which allow the tourist flexibility of itinerary, yet include all the major lakes and many of the tarns (small lakes), mountains, rivers and waterfalls, with mention of places of interest en route. The third section is devoted to a comprehensive gazetteer of all the major towns and many of the villages. For easy reference, places and persons of special importance at certain times appear in heavy type.

CUMBRIAN COASTLINE

Extending for over 193 km (120 ml) from Morecambe Bay to the Solway Firth, the long sandy beaches of this coast are interspersed with towns and villages of great interest. At **Grange-over-Sands,** a popular resort of Southern Lakeland on the shores of Morecambe Bay, the sea recedes over the sands at low tide until almost out of sight. Visitors are advised not to wander far from the shore and the oversands route to **Hest Bank,** north of Lancaster, from **Kents Bank** should on no account be

undertaken without the official guide who can be contacted at Guide
Farm, Cart Lane, Grange-over-Sands. Extensive marshlands surround
the headland around **Cark-in-Cartmel,** but the villages of **Bardsea,
Aldingham,** and **Goadsbarrow,** on the eastern coast of the Furness
Peninsula, afford excellent bathing. Launching facilities are available
for small boats at Rampside on **Roa Island,** the northern coast of
Walney Island and from a public slipway under Jubilee Bridge,
Barrow. The south coast of Walney Island has miles of sandy beaches
with safe bathing; at the northern end, sandhills make excellent
suntraps, whilst the south of the island is protected as a nature reserve.

Although many footpaths are marked as crossing **Duddon Sands,**
they should be traversed with the utmost care. From **Haverigg** and
Millom, opportunities for sand yachting are excellent; the hard sand is
also safe for bathing. Many tracks from the A595 coast road may be
followed to the unspoilt and peaceful beaches between **Silecroft** and
the ancient port of **Ravenglass;** small craft can also be launched from
these two villages. This area of coastline is contained within the Lake
District National Park.

St Bees is a popular small resort with pebble and sandy coves at low
tide beneath towering red sandstone cliffs which form a natural habitat
for many species of sea-bird. Once a small fishing village in the estate of
Sir Christopher Lowther, **Whitehaven** has developed into a port of
considerable size, with many historical associations. Sir Christopher
exploited the coal-mining industry which proved to be the mainstay of
the town in the 17th century. Export to Ireland necessitated the
construction of a harbour, where, at one time, 200 sailing ships were
seen at anchor. Merchants within the town established trading
connections with Virginia and Maryland in 1675, which prospered until
the American War of Independence. In the churchyard of the old church
of St Nicholas, almost completely destroyed by fire in 1971, is the grave
of George Washington's grandmother.

On the cliffs at **Moresby,** a small 19th-century church has been built
with fine views of the Irish Sea. Between the churchyard and the path
leading to the beach is the site of a Roman fort, dating from AD 130.
Nearby **Workington,** with a busy harbour for coasting and foreign-
going vessels, is another town to prosper by the discovery of coal and
rich iron ore within the immediate vicinity, necessitating the
development of ship-building industries. The town's history is
inextricably bound with the Curwen family, who claimed descent from
Malcolm II of Scotland and Ethelred the Unready of England. In the
14th century, they built Workington Hall, a pele tower, altered and
extended by subsequent generations. In 1568, Mary, Queen of Scots
spent a night here during her flight from Scotland. Isabella Curwen
broke the continuity of the male line in 1780 and eloped with John
Fletcher Christian, of the *Bounty* fame. Today, the appearance of the
hall is late 18th century; it is not open to the public and is in a poor
state of repair. Off Ramsey Brown, the charming Portland Square was
laid out in 1775 and is one of the oldest parts of the town.

Beyond Flimby (the site of a Roman signal station) lies **Maryport,** an
industrial, stone-built town of the 18th century, with a small harbour,

situated at the mouth of the River Ellen. It is near the Roman fort of
Alava, parts of which can still be seen. There are magnificent views,
especially from **Seabrows,** across the Solway Firth to Scotland.
Between Maryport and **Rockcliffe** 79 km (49 ml) of coast have been
designated as an area of outstanding natural beauty. **Allonby** and
Mawbray are both small seaside villages where the beaches are backed
by low cliffs interspersed by whitewashed cottages. Here again the
views across the Solway can be unbelievably beautiful, especially at
sunset. Between the villages, the area of **Salta Moss** is a breeding
ground for black-headed gulls. The town of **Silloth** is gaining popularity
as a seaside holiday resort, with broad streets, a large open green, pine
walks and wide expanses of silver sand. North of Skinburness, where
the original town was swept into the sea in 1301, is **Grune Point**—a
shingle spit projecting into the Solway—popular with ornithologists
and, according to legend, where King Arthur's knight Sir Gawaine
encountered the Green Knight.
The 'new' village of **Newton Arlosh,** situated on Moricambe Bay,
was created in 1304 by the monks from Holm Cultram, with an ancient
fortified church. The pele tower will be seen to have no external door,
entrance being gained from the first floor within the church.

Recent excavations at **Kirkbride** have shown evidence of a 30–40-
acre Roman camp dating from AD 70–120, perhaps an extension of
Hadrian's Wall. At the tip of the promontory, **Bowness-on-Solway** is
at the lowest point where it is possible to ford the estuary at low tide, a
crossing which was often made by border raiders. Visitors are,
however, advised not to undertake the crossing or to swim anywhere
near the estuary at ebb tide. Site of the most westerly of Hadrian's
forts, many of the buildings, including the church, have been built with
stone from the Roman Wall. At nearby **Glasson,** the local industry is
haaf fishing—the fishermen standing against the incoming tide with
wide nets into which the fish swim. On the marshes just outside the
village of **Burgh-by-Sands,** King Edward I died in 1307. He lay in state
in the ancient church dedicated to St Michael, and is depicted in one of
the windows. The last point on the Cumbrian coast before it joins the
Scottish border is **Rockcliffe Marsh** at the head of the Solway,
designated as a nature reserve and breeding ground for many types of
gull, cormorants and waders. Permits are available free of charge in
advance from Mr R. Stokoe, 4 Fern Bank, Cockermouth.

CLIMATE

The Cumbrian weather is as varied and changeable as the scenery,
providing a moving kaleidoscope of mood and colour. Grey, lowering
clouds which creep silently down the fells can suddenly vanish, filling
the valleys with bright sunshine. As the presence of high mountains is
indicative of rain, it is not surprising that in a small central area
amongst the highest peaks of Borrowdale lies **Seathwaite,** the wettest

inhabited place in England, with an annual rainfall in excess of
3800 mm (150 in). However, at Keswick only 15 km (9 ml) away this has
dropped to 1400 mm (54 in) and on the leeward side, Penrith has only
870 mm (34½ in). After rain, the visitor is richly rewarded by the sight of
the waterfalls in full flood, notably **Lodore, Skelwith** and **Aira Force.**
In winter, snow is present on the mountains above 500 m (1600 ft) for
approximately 50 days, and on the peaks above 800 m (2500 ft) for
approximately 100 days, whilst in the valleys, many of the smaller
tarns and lakes freeze over affording fine skating. A local phenomena is
the *helm wind,* a cold current of air from the Pennines which blows
down the Crossfell escarpment and suddenly ceases before re-
appearing in the Eden Valley. The western coast enjoys a more
temperate climate, and Grange-over-Sands is said to have the mildest
winter in the North of England. This coastal region has a high annual
sunshine record of over 1500 hours, slightly higher than the interior
lowlands and open valleys, which in turn are sunnier than the
mountainous regions.

LAKELAND HISTORY

The area's history can be traced from approximately the fourth
millenium BC when Neolithic tribes farmed the lower limestone areas
of the west coast. From Walney Island to Drigg, and especially the
sandy promontories of the Esk estuary, extensive finds of waste flake
and tools indicate settlements. At **Pike of Stickle,** Great Langdale,
there is evidence of a large Stone-Age axe factory having traded tools
throughout the country. Rejects have been found in the scree, enabling
identification of the flint. Major Neolithic and early Bronze-Age
settlements can also be detected on the plains and limestone hills of
Furness and in areas surrounding the Eden and Derwent Valleys, with
17 associated sites of stone circles and standing stones. The most
famous are at **Castlerigg,** near Keswick, where 38 stones form a circle
33 m (110 ft) in diameter; and England's second largest circle, **Long
Meg and Her Daughters,** at Little Salkeld: here 59 stones are
contained in a circle 364 m (1200 ft) in circumference. Of the Iron Age,
Carrock Fell is believed to be the only hill fort site in Lakeland, with
scant evidence of lowland dwellings.

    Roman occupation of this most northerly outpost of a vast empire
occurred in AD 71. Continual raids by the Scots emphasised the need
for a frontier defence, and to this end Emperor Hadrian built his famous

Derwent Water across to Lodore

wall, from **Bowness-on-Solway** to the Northumbrian coast. To further
overcome the threat of invasions, coastal forts were constructed at
Moresby and **Maryport** with a major port at **Ravenglass.** The
garrison stationed on **Hardknott Pass** protected the southern marches
and the road to Ambleside. Roads connected the coastal forts to the
station at **Papcastle,** the Carlisle garrison, or Penrith. From
Brougham, High Street completed the network to Ambleside,
effectively containing the unfriendly Brigante tribes in the heart of
Lakeland. By the end of the 4th century, the Roman legions had been
withdrawn. The land passed through successive occupation by the
Celts, Angles and Vikings, many place names and rivers being derived
from these periods.

From the 5th century, Christianity began to penetrate the region. The
exquisite, 7th-century, early-Christian cross at **Bewcastle,** one of the
finest examples in Europe, has carving and scroll work showing the
great craftsmanship of the period. Viking crosses are to be found at
Gosforth, Beckermet and **Penrith.** Many later examples, together
with hogback tombs, lie in churches throughout Cumbria.

At the time of the Norman conquest of Southern England, Cumbria
was occupied by the Scots under Malcolm III. In 1092, William II
marched on Carlisle, routing the Scots and strengthening the garrison.
However, skirmishes continued throughout the Middle Ages until the
Union of 1604. The final battles were fought during the 1745 Jacobite
Rising. During the Norman period, the counties of Cumberland,
Westmorland and Lancashire were formed, each with their individual
baronies. With the continued spread of Christianity, numerous
religious orders sited their monasteries throughout the region,
combining practicality with scenic beauty. They amassed great wealth
and power, being forerunners in the wool trade and major exporters of
stone and coal and many castles were built for their protection, which
with those of the baronies, eventually surrounded the district. Evidence
of these strongholds can be seen at **Dalton, Millom, Egremont,
Cockermouth, Carlisle, Penrith, Brougham, Appleby, Brough** and
Kendal. From the 13th century, there was extensive building of keeps
or pele towers. Here villagers took refuge from the advancing Scots
armies and cattle raiders. Usually three storeys high, the ground floor,
where the livestock was herded, was barrel-vaulted and windowless. A
spiral staircase gave access to the first-floor communal hall with a
fireplace; the upper floor was set aside as a ladies bower. The most
perfect example of a free-standing tower is **Dacre Castle** which can be
viewed by appointment. Of the hundred or so of these towers still
standing, many have been incorporated into mansions, halls and
churches. Early examples are to be found at **Sizergh Castle, Yanwath**
and **Isel Halls.**

The era of the Tudors and the Dissolution of the Monasteries in the
16th century changed the life of the Cumbrian peoples. No longer
dominated by the monks, the small landowner—yeoman farmers known
locally as 'statesmen'—emerged. Tudor architecture became apparent in
the use of round chimneys; **Nether Levens** and **Dalegarth Hall** are
good examples. Elizabethan mullioned windows remained as at **Lorton**

Hall; Hutton-in-the-Forest, Penrith, saw the introduction of long galleries.

The 17th century saw the birth of the Quaker movement at **Swarthmoor Hall,** and many towns and villages contain Quaker Meeting Houses built at this time. On **Birker Fell** near Devoke Water, traces of another Quaker settlement can be found. An excellent example of Georgian architecture can be seen at **Rusland Hall** near Newby Bridge.

By the 18th century, the wealthy landowner wielded power in the area, names such as Lowther, Howard, Strickland and Pennington coming to the fore, with great country mansions evolving from earlier pele towers, many assuming the title of 'castle.' These in turn gave way to more homely buildings. As the people became aware of their picturesque surroundings, aspect became important.

HISTORIC BUILDINGS

The Great Monasteries and Abbeys

During the 12th century, ten monastic foundations were established in Cumbria; five of these retain parish churches which are still in use. With abbeys at Furness, Calder and Holm Cultram, those wielding the greatest power and wealth were the monks of the Cistercian Order. Evolved from a group of Benedictine monks wishing to lead a stricter and more austere life, they founded their abbeys in lonely places, achieving beauty by the simplicity and fine proportions of their buildings. Their habits, basically utilitarian, were of undyed wool, giving rise to the name the White Monks. Grey Monks of the Order of Savigny established their first house in England at **Furness** in 1124 and merged with the Cistercian Order in 1147. In a wooded valley known as Beckonsgill, or 'Vale of the Deadly Nightshade', they built their abbey of red sandstone, now one of the finest monastic ruins in the country, with exceptional examples of Norman workmanship. The east end, belfry tower and transept were extensively repaired in the 15th century and these, together with the cloisters, dormitories and refectory, are open to visitors. The 14th-century infirmary chapel is now a comprehensive museum. A daughter house was founded seven years later at **Calder Abbey** (Seascale). Parts of the nave, tower and north wall still stand to a great height showing the graceful proportions of the church. **Holm Cultram Abbey,** established by King David of Scotland as a daughter house to Melrose Abbey in 1150, was, when completed in 1192, larger than Carlisle Cathedral. Continued Scots

Furness Abbey   *Cartmel Priory, opposite*

raids caused severe damage and by the 16th century the abbey was in
decline. At the Dissolution, Cromwell was petitioned for the
preservation of the abbey, which served as parish church and refuge
against the Scots. The petition was upheld. A considerable amount of
early Norman work can be seen in the present church which occupies
part of the original nave.

Carlisle, Cartmel and Lanercost priories were founded for
Augustinian cannons; Carlisle in 1122, after a visit to the town by
Henry I, Lanercost 44 years later and Cartmel in 1188. By 1133, the See
of **Carlisle** was created, at which juncture the priory achieved the
status of cathedral, the first house in England to do so. A disastrous
fire in 1292 necessitated rebuilding which continued until the late 14th
century; the original grey Norman stonework blending into the red
sandstone of this later period. Henry VIII bestowed an endowment
charter on the cathedral in 1542, transferring most of the priory
possessions to the chapter together with those from the dissolved
Wetheral Priory. Within the cathedral precincts, fragments of the
priory buildings can be traced; the refectory, which survived the
Dissolution is to the south of the cloisters and now houses the
cathedral library. At **Lanercost,** the original nave, with a fine west
door has been continually used as a parish church. A wall across the
east end divides it from the extensive abbey ruins which still retain
almost their full height. In good repair is the $30\frac{1}{2}$ m- (100 ft) long,

vaulted underloft of the refectory, and the western range converted
by Sir Thomas Dacre into his home in the 16th century. **Cartmel
Priory** also survived the Dissolution in 1537, part of the south aisle
remaining in use as the church. Of great structural interest, the
imposing building still retains the original monastery walls.

At **St Bees,** the parish church is contained within ancient priory
walls. Together with Wetheral, the abbey was established by the
Benedictine Order between 1117 and 1120. St Bees stands on the even
earlier foundation of a 7th-century nunnery. The Norman building was
constructed of red sandstone and fine and unusual examples of
12th-century work have been incorporated into the present church.
Scant remains of other priory buildings can be traced to the south.
Wetheral (Carlisle) suffered considerably from continuous Scots raids
necessitating restoration in the 15th century; all that has survived from
that period is the gatehouse. Another abbey to suffer similarly was
Shap, founded at the end of the 12th century for cannons of the
Premonstratensian Order. The striking west tower, remains of the
cloister foundations and communal warming rooms, where there are
stone benches round the walls, form the major part of the ruins seen
today. Virtually nothing is left of the original **Connishead Priory,**
except for the small oratory where prayers were said for travellers
undertaking the dangerous oversands route across Morecambe Bay.

Other interesting churches in Lakeland are described elsewhere in
the book. Relics from Roman, Celtic, Norse and Norman periods will be
seen incorporated into later buildings, many of which have much older
foundations.

Castles

The turbulent years of the Scots raids necessitated the building of
castles and pele towers throughout the county for the protection of the
inhabitants and their livestock. Many of these survived the fierce
fighting and remain intact, whilst others suffered severe damage, later
falling into decay and ruin. Their desolate appearance and stone walls,
sometimes over 2 m (7 ft) thick are grim reminders of those troubled
times. Substantial remains will be found at **Brougham** (Eamont
Bridge). The 14th-century outer gatehouse is almost complete, with a
guardroom over vaulted dungeons and two stories of living quarters
above. A passage leads to the inner gatehouse and the oldest part, the
keep or Pagan Tower, built about 1180. Only the 13th-century east wall
remains of the great hall. It was in this castle that Lady Anne Clifford,
restorer and benefactoress of many Cumbrian churches and castles,
died in 1676.

The strength of **Brough** (Appleby) may be detected in the stately
ruins of which parts of the Norman keep, curtain wall and great hall
are standing. Acquired by the Lords of Clifford in 1204, it was also
restored by the Lady Anne. Both of these castles are in the care of the
Department of the Environment, as is **Carlisle Castle.** Here much of
the building retains its original form although suffering almost total
destruction during the border raids, and changing hands many times.

It was restored using stones from the Roman site at Stanwix. The Regimental Museum of the Border Regiment is housed in the keep. At **Cockermouth,** in private ownership, guided tours are arranged through the interesting ruins which include the *oubliettes*, or secret dungeons and the Mirk Kirk—dark chapel.

Recent excavations have been carried out at **Kendal,** where parts of the curtain wall and three of the towers are all that remain of the stronghold presented to Sir William Parr by Richard II. **Kirkoswald,** a once gracious but small castle with superb views over the Eden Valley, was allowed to fall into decay in the 17th century. A high turret containing a damaged spiral staircase together with fragments of two tunnel-vaulted towers and the gatehouse are all that can now be seen. However, one of the magnificent timber ceilings was removed and is preserved at **Nawarth** (Carlisle). **Pendragon** (Appleby) is reputed to be the legendary home of Uther Pendragon, father of King Arthur. The 12th-century pele tower suffered great pillaging and destruction by the Scots. Rebuilt during the 14th, 16th and 17th centuries, only scant remains can now be found. At **Egremont** the gatehouse, traces of domestic buildings and parts of the 13th-century great hall are still standing. **Penrith Castle** has been allowed to decay since 1550, the crumbling walls, some still retaining a great height, now encompass a public park. Access to these castles is free, although not always easy to obtain, sometimes necessitating a walk across fields; while the picturesque ruins of **Piel Castle,** built as a defence by the monks of Furness Abbey, can only be reached by boat. At **Dalton,** also built by the monks, the massive square tower has survived; now owned by the National Trust it houses a small musuem. **Millom Castle** has been incorporated into a farmhouse, and can be viewed from the road.

Bearing the title of 'castle' are some of the greatest mansions of Lakeland. In most instances they include 14th–16th-century additions to crenellated pele towers. **Appleby** and **Rose** (Carlisle) Castles are in private ownership and not open to the public. At **Nawarth, Dacre** and **Corby** (Carlisle) parties can be shown round by previous written appointment. Also private residences are **Muncaster** (Ravenglass) which stands on a Roman site overlooking the Esk Valley, open three days a week; and **Sizergh** (Levens) owned by the National Trust and open on Wednesdays.

Houses and Gardens

Many of the houses open to the public are furnished as they would have been at the turn of the century and include priceless treasures lovingly collected over the years. Together with the unchanging views of fell and lakes to be seen from the windows, the visitor has the distinct feeling of stepping back in time, and this applies particularly to the houses associated with the poets and writers. A simple Georgian façade hides the warmth contained within the house where William Wordsworth was born at **Cockermouth** in 1770. Here visitors can see the small room to the left of the hall, used as a dining room, and mount the polished wooden stairs to the comfortable upper drawing room looking on to the river, and the terrace where the children used to play. At **Dove Cottage** (Grasmere), where William lived with his sister Dorothy and later brought his wife Mary, the rooms with their original stone-flagged floors and low ceilings have been furnished with many pieces from **Rydal Mount,** the poet's later home. Here too are slate floors and oak beams dating from 1550 when the house was built. Wordsworth enlarged and 'modernized' Rydal for his family, who lived there for 37 years, much of its charm having been retained. Even the gardens are laid out in their original form.

Brantwood, an attractive, long, whitewashed house standing on the wooded eastern shore of Coniston Water, was the home of John Ruskin. In the study are the bookcases, desk and armchair he used in his declining years. The house is now an art gallery containing over 200 of his paintings together with some by Turner and other Lakeland artists. Not far away is **Hill Top,** the little 17th-century grey-stone cottage with its slate roof, tucked away from sight behind the Tower Bank Arms at Near Sawrey. Beloved home of Beatrix Potter, the visitor can easily imagine those immortal creatures, Tom Kitten, Jemima Puddleduck and Pigling Bland in situations so well described and drawn in her books. Everything is just as she left it, and although the view from the farm or down the lane may have changed a little, much remains the same.

Several larger houses have passed through generations of Lakeland's most famous families. These include **Holker Hall** (Cark-in-Cartmel) where the Cavendish family—the Dukes of Devonshire—have been in residence since the hall was built in the 16th century. The Victorian Wing is open to the public and includes the library, drawing room, dining room, main hall and staircase with magnificent oak carving.

Lorton Hall (near Cockermouth) has even older connections, having passed through successive generations of the Winder and Dixon families since Norse times. In common with the majority of great Lakeland houses, a structural feature is the incorporation of a pele tower. Internally the house has extensive oak panelling which blends well with the Jacobean and Carolean furniture. Building on to an existing pele tower, Lord Thomas Dacre founded **'The College'** (Kirkoswald) in 1523. After the Dissolution of the Monasteries, the property was acquired in 1590 by Henry Featherstonhaugh, and it is still owned by the same family. Much of the building seen today is of the 17th century and retains a stone floor and a wealth of carving on original beams, panelling, chimney-piece and staircase. **Hutton-in-the-Forest** (Penrith), **Whitehall** (Mealsgate) and **Hutton John** (Dacre) are also family homes with ancient foundations. Built round pele towers, the 17th-century additions are of notable architectural interest.

     Holker Hall, top   *Brantwood, Coniston*

Townend (Troutbeck) presents a different type of architecture, being an excellent example of a 17th-century yeoman's house built round an open courtyard. Successive generations of the same family held the tenure from 1525–1943, and many of the furnishings are those accumulated by them. Also Elizabethan is **Swarthmoor Hall** (Ulverston). **Rusland Hall** (Newby Bridge) is Georgian with much period panelling. The owners also display a fine collection of mechanical musical instruments.

Gardens

Lakeland gardens are a source of delight to many thousands of visitors each year offering a panorama of colour combined with scenic background. At Ambleside the **Stagshaw Gardens** are open to the public daily as are **White Craggs Rock Garden,** created on part of Loughrigg Fell, the natural rock formation enhancing the setting of alpine and rock plants from all over the world; the gardens are especially beautiful in spring. **The Lakeland Horticultural Society Gardens** are situated in the grounds of the Leonard Cheshire Home at Holehird (Ambleside), and are noted for rock gardens and the magnificent display of flowering shrubs. They are also open daily. Open to the public daily, except Sunday, from April to October are **Lingholm Gardens** (Keswick) with extensive views of Borrowdale. The woodland setting forms a natural background for the beautiful displays of azaleas and rhododendrons.

A feature of a great number of Lakeland houses is that their gardens are often open to visitors. At **Corby Castle** (Carlisle) the gardens lie beside the River Eden and include many architectural features. Of exceptional interest is the cascade which flows down a series of steps from the lawns to the river; in a basin stands the statue of Lord Nelson placed there after the battle of Trafalgar. From the foot of the cascade is a long walk to a small temple where musical entertainments have been held. The grounds are open every Thursday, Saturday and Sunday from 2–7 pm. The extensive gardens at **Levens Hall,** including the famous topiary garden, are open daily from 10 am–5 pm. **Muncaster Castle Gardens** are famous for their many species of azaleas and hybrid rhododendrons; the extensive lawns and long terrace walk afford panoramic views over Eskdale. Open daily from Easter to June and on Wednesday, Thursday and Sunday in July and August. At **Hutton-in-the-Forest** (Penrith); **Holker Hall** (Cark-in-Cartmel) and **Furness Abbey** (Barrow-in-Furness) the grounds are open throughout the year. Those at **Brockhole** (Windermere) which lie along the lake and at **Rusland Hall** (Newby Bridge) are open daily from Easter to end of October; at **Sizergh** the grounds may be visited on Tuesday, Wednesday and Thursday from 2–5 pm during April to September.

Gilsland
Lanercost Priory
Solway Firth
Nawarth Castle
Bowness -on -Solway
Brampton
Carlisle Castle
CARLISLE
Kirkoswald Castle
A 689
M 6
A 6
A 596
A 686
B 5299
A 594
Isel Hall
Bassenthwaite
Cockermouth
A 66
Cockermouth Castle
PENRITH
A 5086
Penrith Castle
Hutton
Brougham Castle
John
Lorton
KESWICK
Dacre
B 5320
Hall
A 591
Dacre Castle
A 591
5091
Castlerigg
Askham
Stone Circle
B 5289
Glen-
A 5289
ridding
Bampton
Appleby
A 592
Brough Castle
Egremont
Seatoller
Shap Abbey
Seathwaite
A 595
Chapel Stile
Dove Cottage
A 685
Strands
Elterwater
AMBLESIDE
Calder Abbey
Troutbeck
A 6
Brantwood
Brockhole
Coniston
B 5285
Muncaster Castle
A 591
A 685
Ravenglass
A 683
KENDAL
Hill Top
Beckfoot
A 593
Hay Bridge
A 5084
A 684
Nature
A 592
Kendal Castle
Reserve
Sizergh
Lakeside
Castle
A 595
Lowick Hall
Levens
A 5074
Hall
B 5292
Millom
Greenodd
A 5093
Cartmel Priory
Ulverston
Grange
M 6
A 590
-over-
A 65
Sands
Dalton

POETS AND ARTISTS OF LAKELAND

An inspiration to many who know and love the area, the Lake District
was immortalized by **William Wordsworth** in the 19th century, his
poems and sonnets painting in words where his contemporary John
Turner used water colours and oils. Accompanied by his sister
Dorothy, Wordsworth would walk the fells and dales, observing and
writing. Ranking as a masterpiece, Dorothy's 'Journal' depicts not only
daily life, but a feeling for the place in which she lived. **Hartley
Coleridge,** a great friend of the family, resided at Keswick before
moving to live with the Wordsworths at Allan Bank, Grasmere.
Robert Southey, brother-in-law of Coleridge, moved into Greta Hall,
where he lived for 40 years, writing prolifically, but not about the
place in which he lived. Together with **Thomas de Quincey** and
Professor Wilson, the group became known as the **Lake School of
Poets.**
   The artist, **George Romney,** was born at Dalton-in-Furness;
apprenticed to a portrait painter in Kendal, his portraits became
famous and included one of Lady Hamilton. Evidence that **John M. W.
Turner** spent a considerable time touring the Lakes is shown by his
sketchbook. His landscapes include the areas around Coniston, Kirkby
Lonsdale, and Buttermere. Most of his paintings were bequeathed to
the Nation and hang in the National and Tate Galleries, London. **John
Ruskin** was a great admirer of Turner. An author, artist and art critic,
he had strong views on social reform which bore a great influence on
the art and architecture of his time. The last 30 years of his life were
spent at Brantwood, Coniston, where he wrote his autobiography,
Praeterita. **W. G. Collingwood,** his secretary, became an authority on
the Lake District, his knowledgeable books providing valuable works of
reference. It was under his guidance that the 'Lake Artists Society' was
formed.

MUSEUMS

The many museums within the county display both past and present
aspects of Cumbrian life and numerous momentoes of the poets, artists
and writers who made their home here.
Carlisle: *Tullie House* exhibits some of Lakeland's earliest history
with stone axes from the Stone-Age axe factory at Langdale; relics of
the Roman occupation include a famous cauldron, and in the grounds
excavations show traces of the ancient city. A replica of the unique
Bewcastle cross can be seen and there is a comprehensive natural
history exhibition. The castle keep houses the *Regimental Museum* of
the Border Regiment.
Kendal: *Abbot Hall Art Gallery* contains period furniture together
with a comprehensive collection of paintings including some by

Lake District National Park and major geographical features

River Ellen
River Derwent
Bassenthwaite Lake
River Eden
PENRITH
R. Eamont
River Eden
Skiddaw
Whinlatter Pass
KESWICK
Ullswater
Trout Beck
Dawes Water
Derwent Water
Lowther Wild Life Park
Crummock Water
Red Pike
Thirlmere
Helvellyn
River Ehen
Honister Pass
River Lowther
Haweswater
Ennerdale Water
Pillar
River Calder
Great Gable
Grasmere
Kirkstone Pass
River Irt
Scafell Pike
Ryda
Wast Water
Bow Fell
Ellen
AMBLESIDE
Wrynose Pass
Esthwaite
Lake District National Park Centre
River Kent
Hardknott Pass
River Duddon
Coniston Old Man
Grizedale Forest
River Winster
River Kent
Devoke Water
Coniston Water
Windermere
KENDAL
River Gilpin
National Park Boundary

Romney and Turner. The *Borough Museum* exhibits Lakeland history and has an extensive natural history section, whilst the *Museum of Lakeland Life and Industry* displays domestic scenes which give visitors a clear insight into local life in bygone days. A new museum housed in the *Old Grammar School* specializes in early toys and games.

Keswick: *Fitz Park Trust Art Gallery and Museum* shows geological and mineral specimens, a small natural history section together with original manuscripts and first editions and paintings by Turner and Nash. The *Pencil Museum* explains production techniques with examples of fine art work. For enthusiasts there is an excellent *Model Railway Exhibition* housed in the old station.

Coniston: the *John Ruskin Museum* contains geological and mineral specimens collected by the author together with much of his original material. At *Brantwood,* his home, an art gallery has been created with over 200 original drawings and paintings by Ruskin and additional works by Turner, Burne-Jones and Prout, among others.

Hawkshead: the *Courthouse* shows period room settings and displays the industrial life of the area, as does;

Grasmere: the *Wordsworth Museum.*

Millom: *Folk Museum* also depicts local industry with a reconstructed mine and miner's cottage.

Workington: the *Helena Thompson Museum* displays period costumes and room settings.

Specialized subjects are dealt with at;

Maryport: *Netherhall* where a new museum has been created to house the unique collection of Romano–British altars.

Grizedale Wild Life Centre and the *Low Hay Nature Reserve* have museums depicting aspects of deer in natural history and forestry.

Whitehaven and **Barrow-in-Furness** both have small maritime museums.

MINING AND LAKELAND INDUSTRIES

Cumbria is not an area generally associated with mining, but in the 16th century the industry was flourishing. Lead, copper and, in small amounts, iron were mined within the Lake District. In 1561, The Society for Mines was granted royal patronage to encourage production, and miners were brought from Germany to work the lead mines of **Borrowdale** and copper mines in **Coniston.** Here the remains of settling tanks, crushing plants, adits and tunnels driven into the hillside are reminders of the industry. Plumbago, or black lead, extensively mined at **Seathwaite,** supplied the pencil factory at Keswick until 1833. The rich lead mines at **Glenridding** continued in production until 1959, and at **Backbarrow,** a charcoal-burning iron foundry opened in 1711 has only recently closed down. Charcoal was also used in the making of gunpowder at **Sedgwick** on the River Kent, and here the waterwheels which drove the mills can still be found. The extensive woods of the Furness and Cartmel Fells supplied much of the charcoal that was needed. Bobbin mills, also using timber from the coppice woods, can be seen in the **Staveley** area using power provided by the Rivers Kent and Gowan; one is still working. In the Furness district, two mills remain, though not in production, at **Spark Bridge** and **Low Stott Park.**

The woollen industry flourished from the 14th century, spinning and weaving being carried out in cottages throughout the Lake District, many of which retain spinning galleries, erected to make full use of the light. The cloth was sent to the fulling mills before being dyed, and ramblers will often come across these old mills, their waterwheels covered with creepers and in a state of decay.

Modern industry is concentrated on the production of slate within the two main rock areas. Attractive, soft, green slate is quarried from the **Borrowdale** volcanic beds, the blue and grey slate originates from the Silurian formations. The largest quarries of Westmorland Dark Blue slate were started in 1771 and are to be found in the **Kirkby Moor** area. At **Honister,** near the head of the pass, are quarries of green slate which have been worked continuously since 1643. Visitors may visit the sheds to see the slate being split by the 'river' and dressed. The quarry is owned by the Buttermere and Westmorland Green Slate Co. Ltd.

At the **Kirkstone Gallery,** Skelwith Bridge, a permanent exhibition of the various uses of slate is on show.

THE COMING OF THE RAILWAYS

The main line between London and Glasgow, passing through Carnforth, Penrith and Carlisle, was opened in 1864. By the following year, a branch had been laid to Windermere, although it was 18 years later before Keswick was brought within the network. Extending to Cockermouth, a two-way traffic system was operating to the east coast and Durham, carrying pig-iron and coke. The line now terminates at Penrith. The link between Carnforth and Furness constituted a major engineering triumph with viaducts spanning the Morecambe Bay inlets. Two branch lines were laid from Furness, the first, to Coniston, carried copper from the mines and closed in 1957. The other, constructed for tourists, ran to Lakeside connecting with the steamers on Windermere. This too was closed in 1967. However, the Lakeside and Haverthwaite Railway Society have re-opened the section of line between Haverthwaite and Lakeside, which they operate with steam locomotives.

Another branch line is 'the Ratty', affectionately known as 'la'al Ratty', running from Ravenglass to Dalegarth, a narrow-gauge

railway originally constructed to carry iron ore from the mines at
Boot to the coast.

A limited timetable operates on the coastal route connecting Furness
with Ravenglass, Whitehaven, Workington and Maryport before
crossing the north of the region to re-join the main line at Carlisle.

THE COUNTRYSIDE

Hill Farming

Throughout Lakeland visitors will discover many typical examples of
hill farms—grey stone-built farmhouses sheltering in valleys and dales,
the boundaries of in-lying pastures marked by the dry stone walls
which criss-cross the county. Although a few of the farmers keep a
small number of milking cows and store cattle, they are primarily
concerned with sheep and often own vast flocks which can number
many hundreds. Herdwicks are the most popular breed; renowned for
their hardiness they provide wool for carpet fibre and tweed and
excellent mutton. Sheep roam freely over the fells for most of the year,
often wandering far from their own pasture or 'heaf', and the difficult
task of gathering them up, sometimes from high crags or deep ravines,

Honister Pass

is undertaken by the black and white border collies working to the
shepherd's whistled commands. The unique skills of the shepherds and
these truly remarkable dogs are demonstrated at agricultural shows and
sheep dog trials held during the summer throughout the region.

In April the ewes are brought down to the shelter of in-lying pastures
for lambing. This is a particularly anxious time for farmers who have
to guard their flocks against attack by foxes and carrion crows. Before
returning to the fells in mid-May, lambs are given identification marks
with traditional ear punches handed down from Viking times, and
'pop' marks of various coloured dyes on their sides. In July the sheep
are again gathered from the fells for clipping and dipping. During a
Lakeland clipping every farmer helps his neighbour and the shearers
are busy from early morning to late evening. Autumn is the time of
year for Shepherds Meets, when stray sheep are rounded up, identified
by their marks and returned to their owners. The evening provides an
opportunity for drinking and singing and a supper of tatie pot (a dish
of Herdwick mutton and potatoes), apple pie and cheese. Throughout
the winter months sheep remain on the fells, and it is not uncommon
for a severe winter with heavy snows to decimate the flocks, many
animals being buried alive in the deep drifts.

Anyone wishing to gain further knowledge of the Lakeland hill
farmer and his way of life should visit one of the 'Open Days'
organized by the National Trust on one of their farms. These are well
advertised locally and the public are free to attend.

Forestry

The Forest of Cumberland originated immediately after the Ice Age
when dense hardwood forests first became established. These provided
shelter for primitive man, and much later hampered the advancing
Roman legions in their occupation of the county. By the 11th century
these woodlands were the habitat of many animals including red deer,
fallow deer and wild swine. The largest tracts were Inglewood Forest
between Carlisle and Penrith, and Copeland Forest south of Thirlmere.
However, extensive hunting by both the local population and Scots
raiding parties, and negligence on the part of foresters and gamekeepers,
caused their decline, and in 1489 Henry VIII ordered disforestation of
the area. The number of trees was further reduced during the 16th
century when they were felled for charcoal production and local ore
smelting. Early in the 18th century coniferous trees were introduced,
and planting of larch, spruce and pine still continues to the present day.
In 1919, the Forestry Commission established a plantation on the
Whinlatter Pass which was to be the first of many undertaken in
co-operation with private owners and amenity groups. Nowadays, the
most popular species of trees to be seen are Sika and Norway spruce,
Corsican and Scots pine, European, Japanese and Hybrid larch and
Douglas fir.

Industries connected with the original hardwood forests included
swill basket-making from oak, bobbin-making from birch, charcoal
production and ore smelting. With their decline others replaced them,
and now young coniferous trees, up to 20 years old, are felled for

fencing posts, stakes and rustic poles; older trees are sent to the large pulp mills at Workington and Ellesmere Port in Cheshire, and to the Midlands for the manufacture of boxes and woodwool. Butt logs from trees over 50 years old are taken to local mills as sawlogs. Minor ancillary industries are the production of firewood and Christmas trees.

There are further benefits derived from the forests with the provision of water catchment areas, shelter belts for farms, conservation of wild life, and opportunities for the public to enjoy quiet relaxation. An excellent example of the latter is Grizedale Forest where a wide range of amenities is offered. Although arousing deep feelings both for and against their presence, these forests form an important part of Cumbria's economy.

Tarn Hows   *Over page, Buttermere*

Friars Crag, Derwent Water

Nature Trails, Reserves and Wild Life Centres

Considerable areas of the Cumbrian coast are protected as nature
reserves. Of these, the **South Walney Reserve** has the largest mixed
breeding colony of lesser black-backed and herring gulls in England,
and is the most southerly breeding place in the British Isles of the
eider duck. Over 50 other species either breed or can be seen here.
Permits are required for all visits, and the reserve is open between the
hours of 6 am–6 pm. Self-catering accommodation is available.
Application should be made to the Warden, 82 Plymouth Street, Walney
Island, Barrow-in-Furness. At **Ravenglass Gullery** there is one of the
largest colonies of greater black-backed gulls in Europe. Permits must
be obtained in advance from the County Land Agent, Cumbria County
Council, Alfred Street, Carlisle. On **St Bees Head,** the RSPB owns the
reserve which can be observed from the public footpath along the
clifftop. There is no charge and permits are not required.

The Lake District National Park and the National Trust provide
helpful literature on walks and nature trails and arrange guided walks
from Ambleside, Bowness, Buttermere, Coniston, Glenridding,
Hawkshead, Keswick and Rydal from Easter to October. Details may
be obtained from any of the information centres.

In **Grizedale Forest,** the Forestry Commission offer an opportunity
for visitors to see and enjoy the forest. The Wild Life Centre has
displays on the subjects of geology, industrial archaeology and modern
forest industries. Photo–safari (the first to be introduced by the
Commission in the country) and observation hides are special
facilities available for photographers. Other activities include nature
trails and walks, a conservation nursery, angling club, pony trekking,
picnic and camping sites. For further details and bookings apply to the
Chief Forester, Grizedale Forest, Hawkshead. The Theatre in the Forest
(see page 36) offers a unique opportunity to enjoy productions in an
ideal setting.

Nearby is the **Hay Bridge Nature Reserve and Deer Museum,**
where permission to view may be obtained on application to the warden
at the reserve, Low Hay Bridge, Bouth-by-Ulverston. Tel. Greenodd
(022 986) 412. The extensive coppice woods of the region were used to
produce a considerable amount of the charcoal required for iron
smelting in the 18th century. In the reserve, tourists will see a
reconstructed pit-head, collier's hut and a potash pit. The Deer Museum
and associated study facilities are situated in a converted barn and show
the four species of deer found in the area. On one of the nature trails,
the deer enclosure contains the same four species.

Lowther Wildlife Park at Askham, south of Penrith, occupies over
100 acres through which visitors may walk or drive to see the various
species of deer, sheep and cattle, together with varieties of small
mammals, water birds, flamingos and cranes. Picnic areas have been
provided with ample parking and a children's playground. Open daily
from May to September and Sundays only in April and October.

The Lake District National Park

The Lake District National Park covers an area of 2242 sq. m (866
sq. ml) from Caldbeck to Cartmel, Gosforth to Shap, and includes all

the principal lakes and fells. It is administered by the Lake District
Special Planning Board on behalf of the county of Cumbria and the
Nation.

Information Centres include those at Keswick, Windermere,
Bowness, and Ambleside. Here visitors will find a wide range of
helpful literature on walks, places of interest, nature trails and current
events. Several form the starting point for guided walks during the
summer.

At the National Park Centre, **Brockhole** near Windermere,
exhibitions of geology, natural history, old industries and farming are
held in conjunction with the Forestry Commission and the Deer
Society. These, together with illustrated talks and films, help to
communicate to the public as effectively as possible the story of the
Lake District. The centre stands in extensive grounds reaching to the
shore of Windermere, and access is possible by boat from Bowness or
Waterhead (Ambleside) during the summer months.

Tourist Boards

The formation of the **English Tourist Board** has increased the
knowledge of Lakeland and promoted many aspects of the area. Not
confined to the National Park, information is supplied on the whole
county and details of places and activities outside the scope of this
guide may be obtained from the **Cumbria Tourist Board,** Ellerthwaite,
Windermere. Tel. (096 62) 4444.

The National Trust

The National Trust was founded in the Lake District in 1895 by
Octavia Hill, Sir Robert Hunter and Canon Rawnsley from Windermere
(who later became vicar of Crosthwaite Church). The Trust owns many
areas of outstanding natural beauty in Cumbria including peaks in the
Borrowdale Fells, the wooded Claife Heights on the north-west shore
of Windermere, Loughrigg Fell near Grasmere and the wooded islands
on Derwent Water. The Roman site of Galava at Borrans Field,
Ambleside, and the Castlerigg stone circle at Keswick also come under
their jurisdiction, together with houses and castles including Hill Top,
Sawrey, the home of Beatrix Potter, Sizergh Castle, Townend at
Troutbeck, Wordsworth House at Cockermouth and Hawkshead
Courthouse. The Trust controls some of the lakes or open spaces on
their shores, and imposes certain regulations for sailing, boating and
fishing. It has established self-catering accommodation, adventure huts
and camping sites for individuals, families and organized groups. In
conjunction with the Ministry of Agriculture, the Trust organizes
open days or 'Look Ins' on many of its farms during the summer. The
public are free to attend and the days are well advertised locally. For
further details visit the Information Centre at Bridge House, Ambleside;
The Main Square, Hawkshead; Chapel Stile, Grasmere; Lakeside,
Keswick, which are open during the season; or the Regional Office at
Broadlands, Borrans Road, Ambleside. Tel (096 63) 3003.

Membership of the Trust allows free access to any of the properties
under their control. Further details from The National Trust,
Membership Department, PO Box 30, Beckenham, Kent BR3 4TL.

Langdale Pikes

Department of the Environment

Many ancient monuments and buildings are in the care of the
Department of the Environment including, Furness Abbey; Shap
Abbey; Carlisle Castle; Lanercost Priory; Brough and Brougham
castles, and are open at standard hours as follows;

March–April	9.30 am–5.30 pm
May–September	,, – 7 pm
October	,, –5.30 pm (All open until 2 pm on Sundays)
November–February	,, – 4 pm

All other places—Castlerigg Stone Circle; Arthur's Round Table and
Mayburgh Henge, Penrith; Hardknott Roman Fort; Penrith Castle and
the various stations on Hadrian's Wall, are open at all reasonable
times, and at most admission is free.

CUSTOMS

Cumbria's colourful, traditional sports and customs are an attraction
enjoyed by many visitors every year.

Sports meetings possibly draw the greatest crowds, especially those
at Ambleside (Thursday preceding the first Monday in August) and
Grasmere (Thursday nearest 20th August). These meetings include
various athletic events and, perhaps most spectacular of all, *the
guides' race*—a steep climb of 451 m (1500 ft) or more to the top of a
nearby fell, before the frantic dash down the slopes to the winning
tape. *Cumberland and Westmorland wrestling* is another popular
feature, the contestants clad in traditional white stockings and
embroidered trunks. Before the *hound trailing* event begins, a drag or
trail is laid by dragging over the ground an aniseed mixture bound in
hemp, then the hounds are loosed, following the course over Lakeland
walls and ditches. Hound trails are also held independently of the
sports meetings on almost every day during the season, from April to
the end of October, somewhere within the county. They are well
advertised and details can be found in the local press.

The Egremont Crab Fair (Saturday nearest 17th September) dates
back to 1266 and begins with the Parade of the Apple Cart. In the
afternoon there are traditional sports, and in the evening a *Gurning*
competition—contestants place their heads through a horse collar, and
the one with the most distorted face wins.

Rushbearing, an ancient tradition still celebrated at Ambleside (last
Saturday in July) and Grasmere (Saturday nearest August 5th) when
children place garlands of flowers and rushes in the church, dating
back to the time when churches had clay or earth floors. It is the
custom at Grasmere to reward the children with a piece of gingerbread.
Also held at Warcop (June 29th) and Musgrave (first Saturday in July).

Sheepdog trials are numerous, but perhaps the most popular are the
Vale of Rydal (2nd Thursday in August) which includes a Terrier Show,

and the Ullswater Sheepdog Trials, known locally as 'Dogs Day' (last Saturday in August). The Wasdale Head Show and Shepherds Meet (2nd Saturday in October) has competitions for ornamental and best-dressed shepherd's crooks, which are a popular feature. An ancient custom of the dale shepherd which still survives is the counting of sheep in Celtic numerals, namely *yan, taen, tether, mether.*

August was originally the time when farmers travelled to Kendal for the sheep sales, known as gatherings. Recently revived, the **Kendal Gathering,** which lasts for two weeks, now comprises a varied programme of events including lectures, concerts and sports meetings. **Foxhunting,** more than merely a popular sport in Cumbria, ensures that the number of foxes are kept down to protect sheep and lambs on the fells. Hunting is all on foot over extremely rough, open countryside. The packs of hounds are the Blencathra, Coniston, Eskdale and Ennerdale, Lunesdale, Melbreak and Ullswater. Anyone wishing to follow the pack should contact the huntsmen for detailed instructions regarding procedure.
Pace Egging, an ancient play performed on Easter Saturday and Easter Monday, tours Southern Lakeland and Furness.

Old pump in Lakeland village

THEATRES

The **Sir Nicholas Seker's Theatre** at Rosehill, Whitehaven, in the grounds of an 18th-century mansion, has interior design by Oliver Messel and seats 230. A varied programme is presented with artists of international repute. Booking office, 30 Roper Street, Whitehaven. Tel. (0946) 2422. Restaurant facilities are provided, and advance booking is advised for late-night dining.

One of the attractions of the **Theatre in the Forest** is its setting in the midst of Grizedale Forest. Productions at this small theatre include music, drama, lectures, film shows and exhibitions. A piano festival in May attracts many of the world's most outstanding concert pianists. For advance booking apply to Mrs Grant, Deer Close, Coniston. Tel. (096 64) 295, daily 5.30–7.30 pm; F. Houldsworth Esq, Bookseller, Rydal Road, Ambleside. Tel. (096 63) 3388; Post Office, Coniston. Tel. (096 64) 259. For those telephoning, tickets may be sent in advance or collected and paid for at the theatre. Restaurant facilities are provided.

At Kendal, the **Brewery Arts and Community Centre** stages drama, music and folk concerts. A restaurant is attached to the theatre. Booking office is at the Centre, Highgate, Kendal. Tel. (0539) 25133.

The only mobile theatre in Britain, the **Century Theatre,** is centred at Keswick during the summer, and productions provide a varied programme of plays with a modern approach. Booking office, the Moot Hall Kiosk, Market Square, Keswick. Tel. (72282) 0596.

TRADITIONAL LAKELAND FOOD

Wherever the visitor goes in Lakeland, he or she will be sure of a warm welcome, never more so than in the small guesthouses and farmhouses. It is in these establishments that traditional food is most likely to be served. Lakeland dishes are simple, for example, *tatie pot* made from Herdwick mutton, potatoes and onions is a hot-pot dish, once a favourite with **John Peel.** For something a little richer try *raised pie*; shaped like a pork pie and with a pastry case, it is filled at the bottom with fine chopped mutton topped with mixed dried fruit, cinnamon and brown sugar. The final layer includes kidney fat and raisins over which is poured a glass of rum: long, slow cooking produces a richly flavoured dish. *Cumberland sausage*, sold in a long coil, a length being cut to the required amount, make the humble 'banger' of the uninitiated look pale. Freshly caught *char* from the lakes taste even more delicious than trout, and there is a plentiful supply of salmon from local rivers. *Flooks* from Flookburgh and *Morecambe Bay shrimps* must not be forgotten. *Cumberland rum butter*, made from Barbados sugar and Jamaican rum, should be eaten on slices of griddle-baked *haver bread,*

which is still made in some areas. Pots of rum butter can be purchased
in most towns and villages, as can the famous *Kendal Mint Cake*, a
sweetmeat rather like a crisp peppermint cream. Other delicacies not
to be missed are *Grasmere gingerbread, Westmorland parkin,
Witherslack damsons* with fresh cream and *Cumberland ham* served
with apple pie and cheese.

TRANSPORT

Bus Services. The main services within the area are operated by the
Ribble Motor Services connecting Carlisle, Penrith, Keswick,
Grasmere and Ullswater. Cumberland Motor Services run to towns
west of a line joining Carlisle, Keswick and Millom. A 'Tour Cumbria'
Ticket allows seven days unlimited travel on Ribble and Cumberland
ordinary buses, in addition to Ribble day and half day excursions
originating from Ambleside, Grange-over-Sands, Grasmere, Penrith and
Windermere. Many other operators offer a comprehensive programme
of full and half-day tours.

National Express Bus Services run daily from many Lakeland towns
direct to the Midlands, London, Luton and St Albans in the south;
Glasgow and Edinburgh in the north; and eastwards to Bradford and
Leeds. Timetables are available from all the companies mentioned and
from Tourist Information Centres throughout the region.

The Mountain Goat mini-bus runs throughout Central Lakeland to
the majority of lakes and passes, either on tour or as a stop-fare bus.
Details of the service and Mountain Goat Holidays are obtainable from
the company at Elleray Garage, Victoria Street, Windermere. Tel.
(096 63) 4341 or 2329.

Railway. The Lake District is served by the electrified main line from
London and Glasgow with through trains or connections from the
whole country. British Rail operate their Motorail service direct from
London to Carlisle from Monday to Saturday inclusive, with a limited
sleeper service between mid-May and the last Saturday in September.
Golden Rail Holidays provide travel from towns all over the country
with accommodation at Windermere, Ambleside and Bowness.
Scheduled Inter-City services call at Grange-over-Sands, Oxenholme,
Penrith and Carlisle with branch line connections for the west coast
and Windermere. Further details are obtainable from all British Rail
Stations, local travel agencies, the AA or RAC, or from British Rail
Midland Region, Elestan House, London, NW1.

Air Services. Limited scheduled flights operate to Carlisle Airport
from Blackpool, Jersey, Isle of Man and London (Luton Airport). Main
airports serving the region are Manchester, Ringway International
Airport; and Liverpool, Speke Airport, from where Hertz Private Car
Hire can be arranged. Advance booking can be made at any local
office or direct to the Hertz Central Reservation Office, 197 Lower
Richmond Road, Richmond, Surrey. Tel. (01) 876 0484.

Steamer Services. Sealink, British Rail, operates a vehicle and passenger ferry service from Ferry Nab, Bowness across Windermere to the B5285 for Hawkshead and Coniston. Cruiser services also run between Lakeside, Bowness and Waterhead (Ambleside). For further particulars apply to the Manager, Lake Windermere Services, Lakeside, Newby Bridge, Ulverston.

On Derwentwater, launches of the Keswick-on-Derwentwater Launch Co. Ltd, ply between Keswick, Ashness, Lodore, High and Low Brandlehow and Hawse End in a clockwise direction, returning to Keswick. Details available from the company, 29 Manor Park, Keswick CA12 4AB. Tel. (0596) 73013.

The Ullswater Navigation and Transit Co. Ltd, runs regular motor yacht services throughout the season on Ullswater, calling at Glenridding, Howtown and Pooley Bridge, and will supply additional information on request. Details from its office at 13 Maude Street, Kendal.

ACCOMMODATION

Lakeland offers visitors a comprehensive range of accommodation from luxury hotels with private swimming pools, to simple youth hostel accommodation ideally suited to walkers, rock climbers and mountaineers. The majority of hotels will be found in Central Lakeland—Windermere alone has over 60 hotels and guesthouses. Other centres are Ambleside, Keswick, Cockermouth, Grasmere and Ullswater, complemented by the periphery towns of Appleby, Carlisle, Grange-over-Sands, Kendal and Silloth. Charges per night for a single room, bed and breakfast, vary from £11.60 at the most luxurious hotels to £1.50 at small guesthouses. Of special interest to motorists are the motels at Cockermouth, Carlisle (2), Keswick and Windermere.

Farmhouses offering dinner, bed and breakfast are especially popular with families who have young children. They appreciate the less formal atmosphere, home cooking and the opportunity of seeing farm animals at close hand.

Self-catering holidays are available throughout the region in cottages, holiday chalets, flats and caravans. Details of these, together with hotel, guesthouse and farmhouse accommodation will be found in a booklet *Where to stay in English Lakeland*, published by the Cumbria Tourist Board and on sale at Information Centres.

The National Trust own holiday cottages at Eskdale, Low Hallgarth, High Hallgarth, Windermere, Tarn Beck, Wasdale and Low Yewdale, which are equipped for up to six persons. There are holiday chalets at Fell Foot, Windermere; furnished caravans at Low Wray; and adventure huts at Keswick, Loweswater, Little Langdale and Coniston. Further details of National Trust accommodation may be obtained by writing to the Bookings Secretary, Broadlands, Borrans Road, Ambleside or Tel. (096 63) 3003.

Dungeon Ghyll Old Hotel

There are over 30 youth hostels situated in and around the National Park. Further details may be found in the Youth Hostels handbook: a regional booklet, *Youth Hostels in Lakeland*; or by writing to the Regional Officer, Elleray, Windermere. Tel (096 62) 2301/2. For family holidays, members with children under 5 years of age can be offered special accommodation in an annexe to the hostel at Buttermere.

All types of holiday accommodation *must* be booked well in advance owing to the exceptional demand at peak holiday periods.

CARAVAN AND CAMPING SITES

There are approximately 70 caravan and camping sites in Cumbria, excluding those under the jurisdiction of the caravan and camping clubs, farmers who, as country landowners, allow caravans and tents on to their land (permission must first be granted here) and the National Trust. The large sites catering primarily for static caravans sometimes have limited pitches for touring caravans and tents. *Where to stay in English Lakeland*, published by the English Tourist Board gives details of these sites; available from local Information Centres.

The National Trust has established centres throughout the region for caravan and camping holidays. At Fell Foot, Windermere there are a number of caravan pitches which afford an overnight stop only during the season, and at Low Wray, Ambleside there are static caravans for hire. Camping sites for individuals and families are at Great Langdale, Wasdale Head and Low Wray Farm, and sites for groups will be found at Low Wray Farm, Ambleside; Park-a-Moor, Coniston; and Base Camp at High Wray. The National Trust, in conjunction with the Caravan Club and the Lake District Planning Board, are establishing a new site at Park Coppice, Coniston. Further details may be obtained from the National Trust Area Office, Broadlands, Borrans Road, Ambleside. Tel. (096 63) 3003.

A comprehensive list of camping sites is also published by the Lake District National Park Information Service, and may be obtained from Information Centres.

Advance booking is essential for touring caravans as sites fill very quickly and parking in lay-bys is strictly forbidden. Under a new scheme now in operation, caravans entering the National Park are counted, and upon a specific number being reached, those without a booked site are refused entry.

ACTIVITY HOLIDAYS AND SPORTS

The natural features of lakes and mountains provide almost endless opportunities for outdoor leisure activities. Many are freely accessible to the visitor, for others permission must first be granted. Bathing in the lakes must be approached with caution as the water is often extremely cold with dangerous undercurrents. Open-air or indoor swimming pools will be found in many of the towns. For children, the myriads of tiny fish, especially near the steamer piers, are a constant source of delight. There are both seaside and inland golf courses within the area which welcome visitors.

Details of more specialized holiday activities are as follows;

Angling. The rivers and lakes of Cumbria offer excellent sport for a wide variety of both course and game fish, ranging from salmon, trout, eels, pike and perch to the more specialized char found mainly in Windermere. It is essential for all anglers to obtain a rod licence either direct from the Cumbria River Unit, Chertsey Hill, London Road, Carlisle; from local post offices, or shops selling fishing tackle. In some instances this, together with the consent of the riparian owner or angling association, is all that is necessary, but in most cases a permit is also required. As with licences, these are readily available and often give details of which waters may be fished. Local boatmen are most helpful and will readily give advice on where to fish and choice of bait.

There are ideal opportunities for sea angling along the Cumbrian coast for cod, whiting, halibut, bass, skate and tope. Deep-sea fishing can be arranged from Maryport, Whitehaven, Workington, Ravenglass and Haverigg.

Fell Walking and Rambling. Both are enjoyed by many visitors to Lakeland who feel that this offers the ideal way to explore the valleys and dales. Weather conditions can change very quickly on the fells and it is essential to wear sensible clothing and walking shoes or boots, and to carry a good map, compass and a whistle. Always leave details with some responsible person about your intended route, time of return, and inform them as soon as you are back. Further details can be obtained from the Ramblers' Association, 1/4 Crawford Mews, York Street, London W1H 1PT.

At **Hassness Walking Centre** near Buttermere, weekly holidays are available with the services of a guide. Details from Ramblers' Holidays Ltd, Bridge Road East, Welwyn Garden City, Herts.

Gillerthwaite Field Centre, Ennerdale, in addition to walking holidays, also organizes mountain-leadership courses. Details from the centre at Ennerdale, Cleator Moor, Cumbria. Tel. Lamplugh (094 686) 229.

Weekly courses in fell walking are held at the **Storrs Hall Hotel,** Windermere. Contact The Sports Council, 70 Brompton Road, London SW1 1EX. Tel. (01 589) 3411.

Countrywide Holidays Association has centres at Ambleside, Grasmere, Borrowdale and Eskdale for walking and climbing holidays, categorized according to degree of difficulty. Contact the Booking Department, 'Birch Heys', Cromwell Range, Manchester M14 6HU. Tel. (061 224) 2887.

Walking holidays are also organized by the **Lake District Leisure Pursuits Centre,** Windermere (address, page 44) and the **Youth Hostels Association** (address, page 44).

Pony Trekking. Fell ponies have played an important role in Cumbria's history, and the old tracks and pack-horse bridges are reminders of the days when these sturdy animals were used by merchants, miners and smugglers. Today, the routes on the lower fells are used by pony trekkers from centres throughout the county. Treks vary from half-day to full-day or even weekly trails using more than one centre. Some offer accommodation, others will arrange this at nearby hotels, guesthouses, or caravan sites. There are also riding establishments and 'all-weather' riding schools. Advance booking is advisable especially during the summer. For all riding, boots or shoes with heels are essential.

The main centres are at Ambleside, Appleby, Bassenthwaite, Cartmel, Hawkshead, Keswick, Penrith, Pooley Bridge and Windermere. Further details are given in the relevant booklet published by the Cumbria Tourist Board.

Rock Climbing and Mountaineering. Lakeland is one of the main centres in England for the specialized sport of rock climbing, which originated here during the late 19th century. A high degree of danger is involved and climbs should never be undertaken alone. Information and advice may be obtained from the British Mountaineering Council, 70 Brompton Road, London SW3 1HE. Tel. (01 584) 7298.

The Lake District National Park Board, through its full-time Wardens Service, runs weekend Mountain Leadership Introductory Courses for adults wishing to take groups on the fells during the summer. Each course involves four weekends. In addition, two weekend rock-climbing courses are held for those boys and girls who have successfully completed a weekend mountaineering course. Further information is available from the National Park Officer, National Park Office, County Hall, Kendal. Tel. (0539) 21000.

Mountain rescue and search teams are located at Coniston Fell, Keswick, Eskdale, Hallsteads on Ullswater, Cockermouth, Ambleside, Kendal, Patterdale, Penrith, Furness and Wasdale, in close proximity to all the main climbing areas.

During the winter months, skiing is possible on many of the fells including **Great Dun Fell,** Appleby; western slopes of **Helvellyn; Raise;** and the **Kirkstone Pass.**

Boating. There are extensive facilities on many of the lakes and along the coast for hiring boats and launching private dinghies. On Windermere, boats may be hired from Waterhead, Bowness and Lakeside; Bassenthwaite Lake from Peel Wyke Landings: Ullswater

The sport of rockclimbing   *Sailing boats on Windermere*

from Glenridding; Grasmere from Wellfoot Boat Landing; and
Derwent Water from Keswick, Portinscale, and Lodore.

Private dinghies, canoes and rowing boats may be launched from
access points on many of the lakes, and from Derwent Water and
Bassenthwaite Sailing Clubs on payment of a small fee. For those
wishing to sail on Buttermere, Crummock Water, or Loweswater,
application should be made to the National Trust at any of their area
offices. The only launching facilities for power boats are on Windermere
and at Howtown on Ullswater.

Sailing. Holidays are available on Windermere and the Sailing School
of the Royal Yachting Association provides weekly courses of
instruction at Storrs Hall Hotel, Windermere. Further details from its
registered office, Victoria Way, Woking GU21 1EQ.

Also on Windermere, Holidays Afloat Ltd, charter out modern yachts
or motor cruisers fully equipped for on-board living. Details from their
offices at Bowness-on-Windermere. Tel (09662) 3415.

The Coniston Sailing School offers instruction on Coniston Water
at Easter, Whitsun and during July and August. Details can be
obtained from the school, or from the Secretary, 33 Meadow Waye,
Heston, Hounslow, Middlesex. Tel. (01 570) 9715.

Water Skiing. Facilities are provided for water skiing on Windermere
from the Storrs Hall Hotel, where courses are available for both
individuals and small groups. The Lake District Leisure Pursuit Centre
offers courses which include water skiing, sub aqua, and canoeing in
addition to a wide range of land-based sports. Notable among these is
grass skiing, which is becoming very popular. Further details may be
obtained by writing to the centre at Limefitt Park, Windermere. Tel.
(096 63) 2300.

Youth Organizations

The National Scout Caving Activity Centre, Whernside Manor, Dent,
Sedburgh, offers weekly and week-end caving courses all the year
round, including special and scientific courses. Preference is given to
members of Guide and Scout associations. Minimum age 16. Equipment
may be hired.

Outward Bound Schools at Eskdale and Ullswater offer tuition in
climbing, pot-holing, mountain leadership, canoeing, swimming and
fell walking. Details from the Director, External Affairs, Outward
Bound Trust, 34 Broadway, London SW1H 0BQ.

There are approximately 30 Youth Hostels scattered throughout the
region. In addition to the usual facilities, Adventure Holidays for those
aged 16 and over, and Eagle Holidays for boys and girls aged 11–15
years are also organized. These are for one or two weeks' duration and
are centred at Hawkshead, Ambleside, Patterdale, Coniston,
Windermere, Grasmere and Keswick. They range from Grade C walking
holidays to Grade A climbing. There are bird-watching holidays at
Hawkshead, with fieldwork in the nearby Grizedale Forest, and audio-
visual holidays at Kendal. Details from YHA Adventure Holidays,
Trevelyan House, St Albans, Herts AL1 2DY.

CALENDAR OF EVENTS

April	Easter Pace Egging Play tours Lakeland
	Hound Trailing Season opens
May	Cartmel National Hunt Race Meeting (Spring Bank Holiday)
	Fairfield Fell Race
	Lake District Festival every other year alternating with The Mary Wakefield Music Festival
	Ullswater Sports
June	Ennerdale Fell Race
	Holm Cultram Festival of Arts
July	Ambleside Sports
	Ambleside Rushbearing
	Carlisle Agricultural Show
	Holker Hall, Lakeland Rose Show
	Keswick Christian Convention
	Skiddaw Fell Race
August	Ambleside, Vale of Rydal Sheepdog Trials
	Bassenthwaite Regatta Week
	Cockermouth Agricultural Show
	Dalemain, Fell Pony Breed Society Show
	Gosforth Agricultural Show
	Grasmere Sports
	Grasmere Rushbearing
	Grasmere Lake Artists Society Exhibition
	Kendal Gathering
	Kendal, County Show
	Keswick Agricultural Show
	Millom Agricultural Show
	Ullswater Sheepdog Trials
September	Egremont Crab Fair
	Hawkshead Agricultural Show
	Lake District Mountain Trial
	Wasdale Head Show and Shepherds Meet
October	Windermere, Power Boat Grand Prix and Record Attempt Week
	Grasmere Antiques Fair

The Lake District National Park Information Service publishes a monthly list of events, and these are also advertised in the local press.

NEWSPAPERS

Daily

Cumberland Evening News	Northern Lakeland
Cumberland News and Star	Northern Lakeland
Lancashire Evening Post	Southern Lakeland
North Western Evening Mail	Southern Lakeland and Furness
Westmorland Gazette	Southern Lakeland

Weekly

Barrow News	Local distribution
Cumberland News	Northern Lakeland
Cumberland Times and Star	Northern Lakeland
Cumberland and Westmorland Herald	General distribution
Grange News	Local distribution
Keswick Reminder	Local distribution
Millom News	Local distribution
Ulverston News	Local distribution
Westmorland Gazette	Southern Lakeland
Whitehaven News	Local distribution

Further Reading

Portrait of the Lakes	N. Nicholson
Lake District History	W. G. Collingwood
Cumberland and Westmorland Buildings	N. Pevsner
The English Lake District	M. Lefebure
Walking in the Lake District	H. H. Symonds
The Lakeland Peaks	W. A. Poucher
The Lakes	W. Heaton Cooper
The Tarns of Lakeland	W. Heaton Cooper
Guide to the Lakes	W. Wordsworth
The Lake District	Roy Millward and Adrian Robinson

HOLIDAY ROUTES TO LAKELAND

Motorists are advised to obtain detailed itineraries from either of the motoring organizations at their local offices or from head office; in the case of the AA this is Fanum House, Basingstoke, Hants. RG21 2EA. Tel. Basingstoke 20123; and from the RAC Touring Services, PO Box 92, Croydon CR9 6HN. Tel. (01 686) 2525. The Department of the Environment also issues leaflets with details of recognized holiday routes.

The accessibility of Lakeland has increased considerably with the opening of the M6 motorway to Carlisle, 482 km (300 ml) from London, and 151 km (94 ml) from Glasgow. Traffic from the south should leave at Exit 35 for the A6, Grange and Southern Lakeland; Exit 36 joining the A65 from Yorkshire to Kendal and Windermere; Exits 37 and 38 also with access to Kendal; Exit 39 joining the A66 from Appleby and Barnard Castle, Teeside and the A1M to Shap summit and Central Lakeland; Exits 40, 41 and 42 also for Central Lakeland; Exit 43 joining the A69 from Newcastle-on-Tyne to Carlisle and Northern Lakeland. At Exit 44, the M6 is joined by the A74 from Glasgow.

LAKE AND MOUNTAIN TOURS

For the purpose of this guide the touring routes have been centred on two towns; **Ambleside** covering Southern Lakeland, and **Keswick** making an excellent centre for the northern lakes. The tours are, for the most part, contained within the Lake District National Park, and wherever possible, points at which routes intersect have been noted, thus enabling the tourist to vary his or her itinerary. For those who wish to obtain a wider knowledge of the county, mention is given in the Gazetteer section of Penrith, Kendal and Appleby, good centres from which to tour the area between the Lake District National Park, bounded by the M6, and the Pennines. Carlisle, situated to the north of the region, contains many tourist attractions and is the starting point from which to tour the Roman Wall.

It is suggested that visitors obtain a copy of the Ordnance Survey Lake District Tourist Map as an essential accompaniment to this guide; although all main roads are numbered, many passes and minor roads are unclassified.

Ambleside stands at the head of Lake Windermere, ringed by wooded hills with the mountains beyond. Its position at the junction of the busy A591 Kendal to Keswick road, and the A593 to Coniston and the west coast, makes it an ideal touring centre. The waters of Stock Ghyll tumble down the force and pass through the centre of the town on their way to join the River Rothay, which in turns joins the Brathay, at the head of the lake. The small, two-storied house, built on a single-arched bridge over the ghyll is a popular tourist attraction. Originally a summer or apple-house at Ambleside Hall, it is now used by the National Trust as an Information Centre. In addition to the many fine walks around the town which afford superb views of Windermere and the surrounding countryside, there is much for the visitor to enjoy. St Mary's Church, designed by Sir Gilbert Scott in 1850, is famous for the annual Rushbearing Ceremony, held on the last Saturday in July. At Waterhead, visitors may embark on the Sealink cruisers for tours of the lake. Facilities are also available for watersports and boat hire. Ambleside was well known to William Wordsworth who lived at Rydal

Mount for 37 years and to Dr Arnold Fox who made his home at the 'How' on the banks of the River Rothay. In 1835, Hariette Martineau chose the 'Knoll' from which to continue her prolific writing.

Tour 1   Ambleside, Windermere, Coniston and Grizedale Forest
The A591 southwards closely follows the lake shore to Windermere and Bowness and passes **Brockhole,** the Lake District National Park Centre. This 19th-century house, which was opened in 1969, receives thousands of visitors each year, and is described on page 32. Situated on the A592, 1 km ($\frac{3}{4}$ ml) north of the junction with A591, are the Lakeland Horticultural Society Gardens at **Holehird.** The grounds of this Leonard Cheshire Home are noted for rock gardens and extensive displays of flowering shrubs. Open at all reasonable times, admission is free.

Windermere, England's largest lake, is 17 km ($10\frac{1}{2}$ ml) long and $1\frac{1}{2}$ km (1 ml) across at the widest point, and has exceptional depths of up to 64 m (210 ft) with underwater hills and valleys. The twin towns of Windermere and Bowness are indivisible. **Windermere village** is set on a hill, with narrow and sometimes steep alleys giving way to wider main streets and open parklands. The oldest part of **Bowness** surrounds the 15th-century church of St Martin where among the treasures are a 'Beechers Bible' and a collection of chained books. The font top is Saxon and the east window depicts the coat of arms of John Washington, ancestor of George Washington; some of the glass is believed to be from Cartmel Priory.

Bowness lake shore is a busy Sealink terminal, both for the vehicle and passenger ferry to the western shore at Ferry House and for the lake cruisers to Waterhead and Lakeside. Visitors are advised, before taking part in the many watersports available, to obtain a chart of the lake and a copy of *Collision Rules* which have been issued to safeguard the interests of all lake users. Both may be obtained from the Lake Warden, South Lakeland District Council, 'Ashleigh', Windermere. Moorings have been provided by the council at Parsonage Bay and at Ferry Nab where there is also a slipway. Available between Easter and 31st October, bookings and further enquiries should be made to the address above. Water skiing and power-boat racing are popular; the Power Boat Grand Prix and 'Record Attempt Week' being held in October. **Belle Isle,** the largest island in the lake, covering $14\frac{1}{2}$ ha (36 acres) of woodland, is open for four days at Easter and from Spring Bank Holiday to mid-October, every Sunday, Monday, Tuesday and Thursday. Catering facilities are available and cruisers from Cockshott Point operate a regular service.

The full beauty of the lake can best be appreciated from one of the lake cruisers plying from Waterhead via Bowness to Lakeside. On the western shore, Grizedale Forest is seen to merge with the wooded slopes of Claife Heights, while to the east the many fine houses and hotels, including Storrs Hall, headquarters of the Royal Windermere Yacht Club, can be observed set against the wooded background of Great Tower and Gummer's How on Cartmel Fell.

The A592 follows the eastern shore for 14 km (9 ml) to Newby Bridge

Ambleside, routes for Tours 1, 2, 5 and 6
Keswick, routes for Tours 9 and 10
The Ambleside tours take in Windermere, Coniston, Grizedale Forest,
the Langdales, Eskdale and Wast Water, Rydal, Grasmere and Keswick.
The Keswick tours take in Bassenthwaite and Caldbeck, Borrowdale,
Crummock Water and Vale of Lorton.

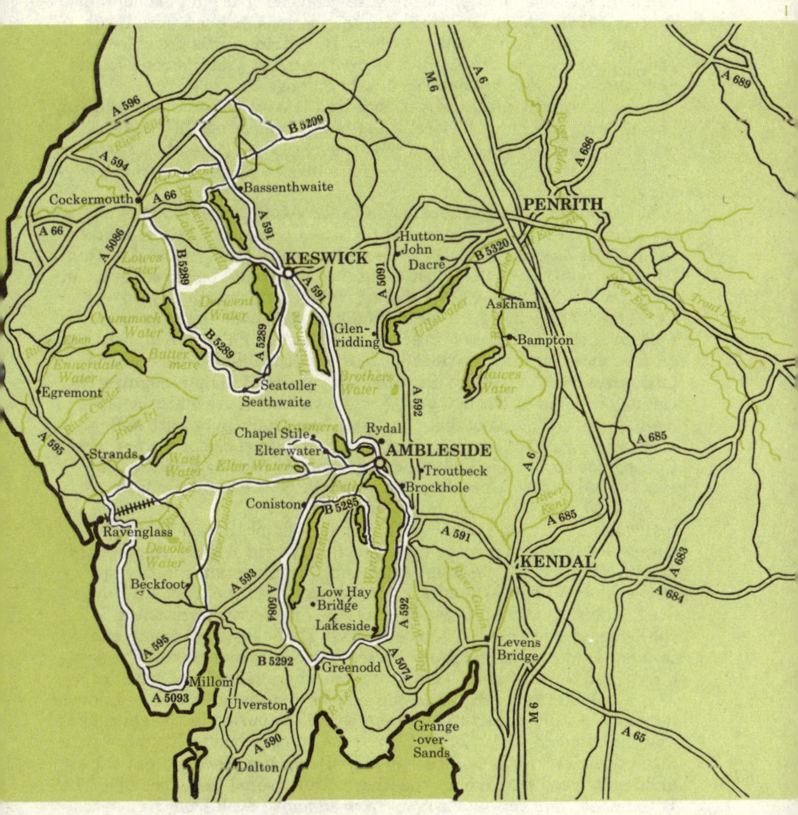

A 596
A 594
A 66
B 5209
A 689
M 6
A 6
A 686
Cockermouth
A 66
Bassenthwaite
PENRITH
A 591
A 5086
B 5289
Hutton
John
B 5320
KESWICK
Dacre
A 5091
A 591
Askham
B 5289
A 5289
Derwent
Water
Ullswater
Lowes
Water
Crummock
Water
Bampton
Butter-
mere
Ennerdale
Water
Glen-
ridding
Thirlmere
Brothers
Water
Hawes
Water
Egremont
Seatoller
Seathwaite
A 592
A 685
A 595
Chapel Stile
Rydal
Strands
Elterwater
Elter Water
Wast
Water
AMBLESIDE
Troutbeck
Brockhole
A 6
Coniston
B 5285
A 591
Ravenglass
A 685
KENDAL
A 593
Devoke
Water
A 683
Beckfoot
A 5084
Low Hay
Bridge
A 592
A 684
Lakeside
A 595
Levens
Bridge
B 5292
Greenodd
A 5074
Millom
A 5093
Ulverston
Grange
-over-
Sands
M 6
A 65
A 590
Dalton

where it joins the A590 from Levens Bridge. At **Fell Foot Park** National Trust facilities include boat hire; slipways for private launching (no motor boats); picnicking; a café; caravan park and self-catering chalets. Bathing in the lake is safe in this area, although a lookout should be kept for boats entering and leaving the upper reaches of the River Leven.

After crossing the river, a detour may be taken to **Finisthwaite** and the walk up to High Dam, similar in many respects to Tarn Hows. Nearby, **Graythwaite Hall** gardens, with a fine display of azaleas, rhododendrons and flowering shrubs are open from 1st April to 30th June from 10.30 am–6 pm daily. Near **Satterthwaite** is the Forestry Commission's Wild Life Centre and Deer Museum. The village of **Rusland** has some fine old farmhouses and the Georgian mansion of **Rusland Hall** which, together with the gardens, is open from Easter–October, from 11 am–6.30 pm. At **Low Hay Bridge** it is possible, by prior application to the warden, to visit another wild life reserve and deer museum. Both are described fully on page 31.

From **Haverthwaite,** the Lakeside and Haverthwaite Steam Railway Society runs a regular service to Lakeside connecting with Sealink cruisers, for which a combined ticket is available. Timetables are obtainable and the line is open for four days at Easter and from early May to October.

At Greenodd, turn northwards on to the A5092 and in 6 km (4 ml) take the A5084 following the course of the River Crake to **Lowick Bridge** (with its disused watermill) and nearby **Lowick Hall,** home of Arthur Ransome—author of the much-loved *Swallows and Amazons* books for children. Joining the A593 in Torver village, turn north east to **Coniston.** There are good views from the road over the lake to the eastern shore, Grizedale Forest and the Furness Fells, which, seen early on a summer morning as the sun rises over the fells to disperse the mist, presents a picture of mirrored tranquillity. Easily recognizable among the trees is **Brantwood,** a whitewashed house which was for many years the home of John Ruskin. Now primarily an art gallery housing over 200 of his paintings, together with those of Turner, Prout, Collingwood and Northcote, the house is also used as a residential educational centre. Open from February to November daily from 10 am–5.30 pm, Saturdays from 2 pm.

It was on the long lake that Sir Donald Campbell died on 4th January 1967 attempting to break his own World Water Speed record of 443 km (276.3 ml) per hour. A memorial to him stands in the square at Coniston village. Watching over the lake from the west are Dow Crag, Coniston Old Man and Wetherlam, all of which present a challenge to walkers and climbers alike. The lakeside camping and caravan sites provide facilities for most watersports and boats may be hired from the Coniston Boating Centre where launching facilities are also available. Few visitors to this old grey, stone-built village know of its many literary associations. John Ruskin is buried in the churchyard and the museum which bears his name also perpetuates his memory. A fascinating picture of his life can be built up from the original works and reproduced engravings, together with personal items brought from Brantwood. The museum is open from 10 am to dusk from Easter to October. Alfred, Lord Tennyson stayed at the 15th-century Coniston

Ambleside, routes for Tours 3 and 7
Taking in the Duddon Valley, Ullswater and Keswick

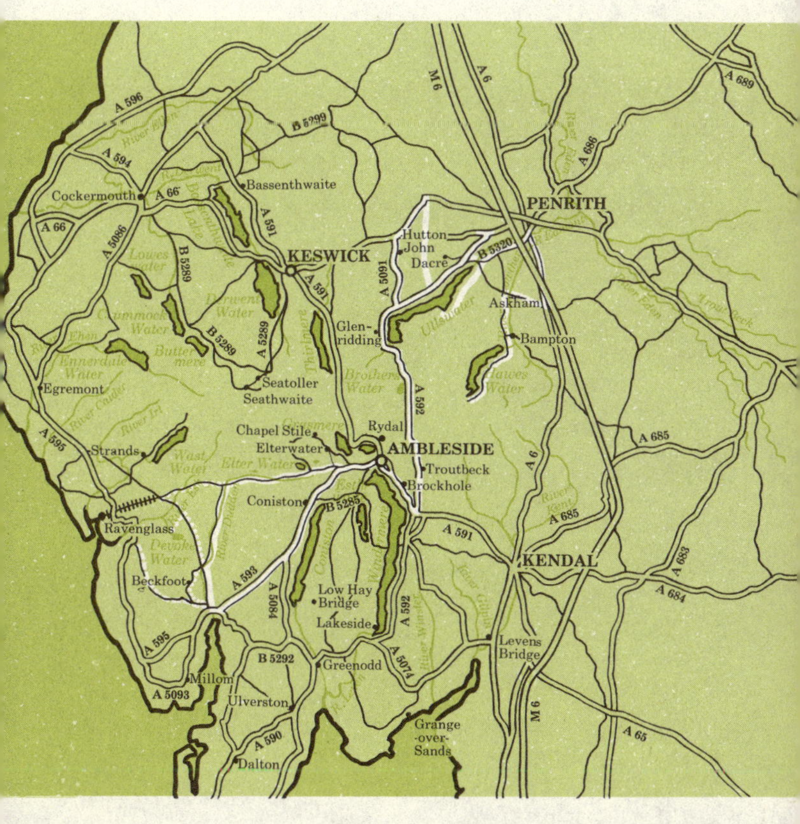

A 596
B 5299
A 594
River Ellen
R. Derwent
Cockermouth
A 66
Bassenthwaite
A 591
A 66
A 5086
Bassenthwaite Lake
B 5289
PENRITH
M 6
A 6
A 689
A 686
River Eden
KESWICK
Hutton
John
Dacre
B 5320
A 5091
Lowes water
Derwent Water
B 5289
A 5289
A 591
Thirlmere
Glen-
ridding
Ullswater
Askham
Crummock Water
Bampton
River Ehen
Butter mere
Brothers Water
Hawes Water
Ennerdale Water
Seatoller
Seathwaite
A 592
Egremont
River Calder
River Irt
Grasmere
Chapel Stile
Rydal
A 685
A 595
Elterwater
AMBLESIDE
A 6
Strands
Wast Water
Elter Water
Troutbeck
Brockhole
River Kent
Coniston
B 5285
A 685
Ravenglass
Coniston Water
Windermere
A 591
Devoke Water
River Duddon
Beckfoot
A 593
Low Hay
Bridge
A 5084
A 592
River Winster
KENDAL
A 683
Lakeside
A 5074
River Gilpin
A 684
A 595
Levens
Bridge
B 5292
Greenodd
Millom
A 5093
Ulverston
M 6
A 590
Grange
-over-
Sands
A 65
Dalton

Isolated Wast Water

Ambleside, route for Tour 4
Keswick, route for Tour 8
The Ambleside tour takes in Millom and the west coast, the Keswick
tour includes Whinlatter Pass and Ennerdale

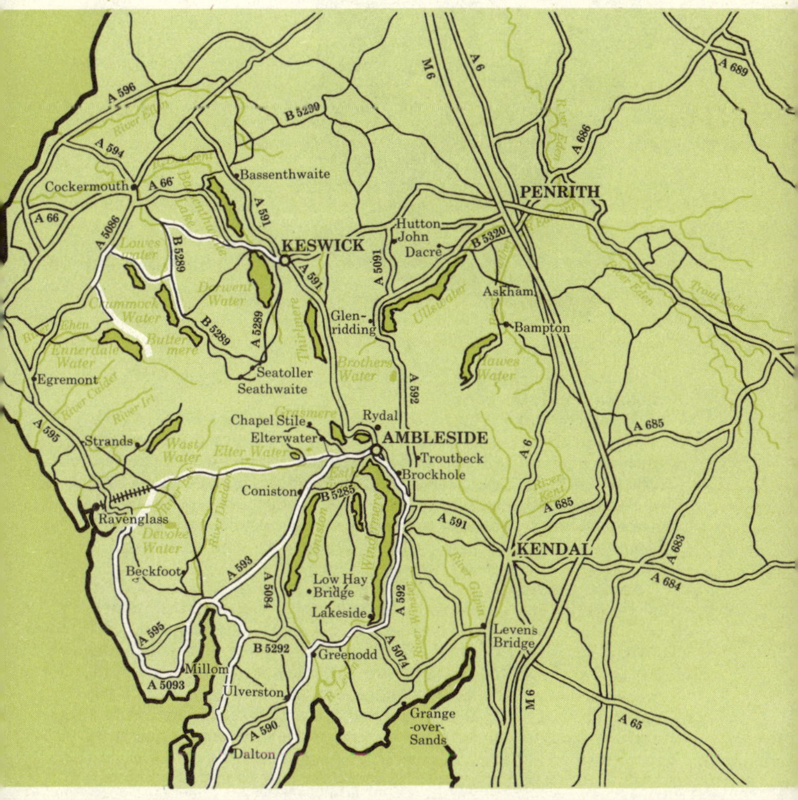

A 596
A 594
B 5299
M 6
A 6
A 689
River Eden
A 686
Cockermouth
A 66
Bassenthwaite
A 591
PENRITH
A 66
A 5086
Lowes water
B 5289
KESWICK
Hutton John
Dacre
B 5320
Crummock Water
Derwent Water
A 591
Askham
Ennerdale Water
Butter mere
B 5289
A 5289
Glen- ridding
A 5091
Bampton
Ullswater
River Eden
Trout Beck
Egremont
River Ehen
River Calder
Seatoller
Seathwaite
Thirlmere
Brothers Water
Lowes Water
River Irt
Grasmere
Rydal
A 592
A 685
A 595
Chapel Stile
Elterwater
AMBLESIDE
A 6
Strands
Wast Water
Elter Water
Troutbeck
Brockhole
River Kent
Ravenglass
Coniston
B 5285
A 591
A 685
Devoke Water
River Duddon
Esthwaite
KENDAL
Beckfoot
A 593
A 5084
Low Hay Bridge
Coniston Water
Windermere
A 592
River Gilpin
A 683
A 595
Lakeside
A 5074
Levens Bridge
A 684
Millom
A 5093
B 5292
Greenodd
Ulverston
River Leven
Grange- over- Sands
M 6
A 65
A 590
Dalton

Anne Tyson's cottage,
Hawkshead, opposite

Hall, and more recently the lake was the setting for the film of
Swallows and Amazons.

For the return journey to Windermere, leave the village by the
B5285 and climb up through woodland for 5 km (3 ml) before turning
onto an unclassified road to **Tarn Hows.** Surrounded by the distant
fells of the High Street range, Helvellyn, the Langdale Pikes and nearer
at hand, Bowfell, the wooded shores of conifer and larch make this
one of the most photographed beauty spots of Lakeland. Served by the
Mountain Goat Bus Service and provided with ample car-parking
facilities, it is also a good walking centre.

At the junction with the B5286 stands the 15th-century Courthouse,
all that remains of the manorial buildings of **Hawkshead,** which
before the Reformation was the judicial centre for the monks of Furness
Abbey. Now the Lakeland Folk Museum, various aspects of Lakeland
life and crafts are shown together with replicas of late Victorian
domestic scenes. Owned by the National Trust, it is open at Easter
weekend; then from May to the end of October, daily, except Monday
and Thursday, from 2–5 pm. Picturesque Hawkshead village with its
whitewashed cottages, narrow streets and cobbled yards was, in the
Middle Ages, an important market town; now the haunt of artists it is

best explored on foot. In the village is Ann Tyson's cottage where
William Wordsworth lodged while he was a pupil at the local grammar
school. The knoll above the town, where the church now stands, marks
the site of an early Norse settlement from which the village obtained
its name, *Haukr's saeter*. Travelling south, pass the ancient Quaker
Meeting House at **Townend** and continue down the east side of
Esthwaite Water, a quiet undisturbed lake whose reed banks are a
haven for wild fowl. It is reputed to be the home of Jeremy Fisher, one
of Beatrix Potter's endearing little characters. **Hill Top,** Sawrey, where
she lived until she married, and then used as a studio, lies to the south
of the road. Open from April to end of October daily from 11 am–5.30 pm.
Sundays from 2.30 pm. The house is administered by the National
Trust and displays drawings, furniture and china as they were left by
the author. Visitors are warned that considerable delays may occur at
peak viewing times owing to the small size of this 17th-century house.
Proceed from here to the ferry and rejoin the A592 in Bowness.

Tour 2   Ambleside and the Langdales

This is a short, circular tour leaving on the A593, past the Roman fort
of **Galava** at Borrans Field. Here a 1st-century fort was overlaid by a
later Hadrianic structure. Excavated relics are on display at **Brockhole**
National Park Centre together with reconstructed layouts. **White
Craggs Rock Garden,** Clappersgate, to the north of the road has been
created on part of Loughrigg Fell and includes many unusual plants
from all parts of the world, which present a particularly beautiful

display in the spring. The gardens are open throughout the year from dawn to dusk. Turn right at the crossroads at Skelwith Bridge for **Loughrigg Tarn.** There is a pleasant walk down the driveway and round the tarn. The lane to the south west can be taken to **Elterwater,** but has steep gradients. Returning to Skelwith Bridge, park the car and walk to **Skelwith Falls,** although only 4½ m high (15 ft), after heavy rain the might of the River Brathay thunders through the narrow gorge. The B5343 passes Elterwater, where the waters of the River Brathay and Langdale Beck merge, and continues to **Chapel Stile,** a village mainly concerned with slate quarrying. Here the road sweeps round beneath the towering Langdale Pikes, where from Old Dudgeon Ghyll Hotel climbers make the ascent of the Pikes and Bowfell. The site of the ancient **Pike of Stickle** stone axe factory can also be seen from here. A sharp right-angle turn starts the steep descent, maximum gradient 1 in 5, interspersed with hair-pin bends, past the attractive **Blea Tarn** with extensive views of the Langdales behind. At Fell Foot, join the lower slope of the Wrynose Pass where it passes Little Langdale Tarn before the junction with the A593 at Colwith Bridge for Ambleside.

Tour 3   Ambleside and the Duddon Valley

Follow the A593 to Coniston, Torver and Broughton-in-Furness. In Broughton, the attractive square, surrounded by fine chestnut trees and where the market is held on Thursdays, has an ancient fish slab, stocks and an obelisk. The church of St Mary retains a fine Norman doorway, although much of the building is Early English in style. Broughton Tower and parts of the dungeons are reminders of the castle built by the Broughton family who settled in the area during Anglo Saxon times. Although the ruins are now part of a school, there are several footpaths leading through the grounds. A short distance from here on the A595 is **Duddon Bridge,** where the beautiful Duddon River enters Morecambe Bay. The tourist now has a choice of routes: **i.** Turning immediately northwards on the east side of the river, excellent views are to be seen of Ulpha Park and beyond, the peaks of Stickle Pike and Caw. In the hamlet of **Ulpha,** the dale chapel of St John has some interesting 17th- and 18th-century wall paintings and bears the royal arms of Queen Anne. Re-cross the river at Hall Dunnerdale and continue to **Seathwaite.** Park the car and walk across the stepping stones to the mouth of the gorge. Here, under the rock face of Wallabarrow Crag, the river tumbles over beds of pebble and slate, a scene immortalized by Wordsworth in one of his sonnets. The valley continues through the Forestry Commission plantations on **Harter Fell** to join the road from Little Langdale to **Eskdale** and Tour 5. Turning immediately eastwards, start to climb steeply to the head of **Wrynose Pass,** 390 m (1281 ft), with maximum gradients of 1 in 3½. The Three Shire Stone on the summit marks the point where the old counties of Cumberland, Lancashire and Westmorland met. The hazardous descent to **Langdale Tarn** offers magnificent views of Langdale Pikes to the north with Helvellyn in the distance and to the south east, wooded fells hiding the lakes of Windermere and Coniston from view. At Colwith Bridge join Tour 2 for the return to Ambleside.

ii. The west side of the River Duddon offers two roads over the fells to Eskdale. At Beckfoot the road divides, the westerly fork leading directly to the A595 coast road at Broad Oak, described in Tour 4. From the summit of the fells, along an ungated road with cattle grids, there are extensive panoramic views along the coast to **Calder Hall** and **Winscale** (United Kingdom Atomic Energy Authority) with St Bees head in the distance.

iii. An alternative route passes behind Ulpha Park before a steep descent into the village, turn north west and climb sharply on to Birker Fell. In 5 km (3 ml) a track leads west towards **Devoke Water,** one of the Lakeland's largest tarns, set in heather-covered moorland and with spectacular views in all directions. It is possible to walk from the tarn to the deserted village of **Woodhead,** once a Quaker settlement and now in ruins. A group of small standing stones by the lake marks the graves of people from the settlement. The descent is made, with steep gradients in places, to meet the Langdale to Eskdale road, described in Tour 5. Turning eastwards, pass through the Esk Valley to join the unclassified road over **Hardknott Pass.** Maximum gradients 1 in 3¼. On a mountain spur at the head of the pass, 393 m (1291 ft) stands **Hardknott Castle,** the Roman fort of Mediobogdum, covering an area of over 1 ha (3 acres). Excavations show gates at the centre of each wall and have revealed the commandant's house, granaries, bath block and parade ground. In the care of the Department of the

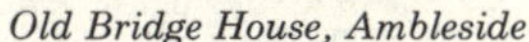

Old Bridge House, Ambleside

Environment, the fort is open at all reasonable times and access is free. The pass continues between Harter Fell and the Steeple, with many hair-pin bends, to join the Wrynose Pass and Tour 3 i.

Tour 4 Ambleside, Millom and the West Coast

Follow Tour 3 to Duddon Bridge and continue on the A595 to Halthwaites, turn due south for **Millom,** a town surrounded by beautiful countryside and sandy beaches. A mile from the town centre, the A5093 passes the castle and Holy Trinity Old Church, both encircled by a moat, traces of which can be detected. In 1335, a fortified stone building replaced the original wood structure which existed before the Norman Conquest. For 500 years the castle was the home of the Hudleston family, Lords of Millom. They held *Jura Regalia*, the power of life and death, over their subjects, and in a nearby field a stone marks the spot where the gallows once stood. The ruined curtain wall, gateway and pele tower encompass a farmhouse and can be viewed from the road. The old church, also built on an ancient site, has some fine examples of Norman work, especially the north doorway. The unique fish window, in the shape of an almond, is 14th century and the font is over 500 years old. In the town, a visit should be made to the recently opened Folk Museum which houses a small geological and natural history section and full-scale reconstructions of a drift of the Hodbarrow Iron Ore Mine, an old smithy and a miner's cottage. Open from 2–5 pm daily, from Easter to September 30th. The Information Centre is also at the museum. Millom Show, held on the last Saturday in August, includes Cumberland wrestling and hound trailing. The attractive village of **Haverigg** offers excellent sands for bathing and sand yachting, there is also a children's pleasure ground and paddling pools.

At the village of Whicham, rejoin the A595 and proceed northwards: several side roads lead to the coast with unspoiled and extensive sandy beaches. Nearing the estuary of the River Esk, a lane goes to **Hall Waberthwaite,** where the original crossing was made to Ravenglass. The low, white church retains an ancient cross shaft fragment from the 10th century, similar to Irton Cross in Eskdale. Continuing on the main road, **Muncaster Castle** soon comes into view across the river: this great mansion, surrounded by wooded fells, is described in Tour 5 which may be joined at this point.

For those visitors not wishing to undertake the Eskdale tour or traverse the passes to Ambleside, the return from Millom can be made by taking the A595 to Broughton-in-Furness and following Tour 3 in reverse order. Alternatively, a detour could be made to include the **Furness Peninsula;** visiting Dalton, Furness Abbey, Barrow and Walney Island, the sandy beaches of the east coast, to Ulverston and Greenodd, here join Tour 1.

Tour 5 Ambleside, Eskdale and Wast Water

The most spectacular way to reach **Eskdale,** the valley of the River Esk, is to approach from Ambleside over the Wrynose and Hardknott Passes; the journey should not be undertaken lightly as gradients

reach 1 in 3 and have many hair-pin bends on a road that is rough in
places, allowing two cars to pass with difficulty. An additional hazard is
created by the sheep which roam freely over the fells, and all access
roads are protected by cattle grids. However, the views obtained are
superb and, after reaching the summit of Hardknott, the tourist is well
rewarded by the panoramic spectacle spread out before him. If time
permits, park the car at **Dalegarth** Station and proceed on foot to
explore the track from the hamlet of **Boot,** following lovely Whillan
Beck, with cascades on the lower reaches, past the ruined mill to
Longrigg cairns and stone circles—41 standing stones enclose five
circles. Just past the station, take the lane to the south leading to
16th-century **Dalegarth Hall,** now a farm, with unusual, round,
Elizabethan chimneys. Follow the path, often muddy, to **Dalegarth
Force** on Stanley Ghyll, a true fall and one of the finest in Lakeland,
plunging 18 m (60 ft) from the overhang. For those who care to, it is
possible to climb to the top and look down on the fall.

The Ravenglass and Eskdale Railway is an interesting 11 km- (7 ml)
excursion to the coast. The narrow gauge track was laid in 1875 to
transport iron ore from the mines near Boot to the coast, and was
converted to the present 381 mm (15 in) gauge in 1917. Steam and
diesel engines are used to pull both open and closed carriages through
the deep gorge at Holling Head before emerging into open fields. It is
possible to park at Ravenglass or meet the train at any of the four
stations en route. By road, proceed in a south-westerly direction
crossing the river and joining Tour 3 iii from Ulpha, follow the river
valley to the junction with the A595, join Tours 3 ii and 4. Re-cross
the river, travelling northwards, for **Muncaster Castle.** In an area
rich in Roman associations, it is not surprising to know that there was
a Roman encampment here in the 4th century. Work began on the stone
castle in the 13th century, incorporating the original pele tower. Major
additions were made in the 15th century and again between 1862–6. In
the main hall, tape transcripts of the castle tour are available in several
languages. Much of the beautiful furniture is of the Charles II and
William and Mary periods. The elegant, octagonal library contains
over 4000 books. Looking from the king's bedroom towards Muncaster
Fell, notice the 'pepper pot' monument, erected to commemorate the
battle of Towton, and where shepherds found Henry VI wandering on
the fells. The King was taken to the castle where he stayed for a while.
In gratitude he presented his host with an engraved green glass bowl,
known as the 'Luck of Muncaster', saying that the family would
prosper if the bowl remained unbroken. The magnificent setting of the
castle and gardens, overlooking the River Esk, are enhanced by
extensive displays of azaleas and rhododendrons for which they are
famous. Also of interest is the wild life park with deer, flamingos and
an aviary. The castle is open from Easter to the end of August on
Sunday, Wednesday, Thursday and Bank Holidays from 2–5 pm, the
gardens on the same days from 1–6 pm. Before leaving the castle
precincts, obtain permission to enter **Walls Castle** from the Estate
Office. Situated down a lane to the south of the road to Ravenglass, on
the bend just before the railway bridge, a walk of about ½ km (¼ ml) is

Walls Castle. Said to be one of the best-preserved Roman buildings in the country, it was probably the villa of the local commander. Four rooms can be clearly detected with the brickwork and arches in an excellent state of preservation, in some cases with original Roman cement.

Ravenglass, a small village beside the estuary, once a Roman trading port, caters mainly for fishermen and from here it is possible to hire boats for day sea fishing. The mud flats are a haven for waders and sea birds. Nearby are the **Drigg Dunes Gullery** described on page 89. Returning to the A595, continue northwards for approximately 5 km (3 ml), take a turning east following the signs to **Santon Bridge.** On the way, visit the church of **Irton** where the churchyard contains a most remarkable 9th-century cross, intricately carved and retaining the head.

From Santon Bridge the road winds through attractive countryside to **Strands,** with its interesting, small dale chapel, bearing the royal arms of George III. The 17th-century panelling and carved lectern are from York Minster. A breathtaking view of **Wast Water** is obtained as the road breaks through the line of trees. The dark, forboding screes plunging into the lake to a depth of 79 m (260 ft). Forming a backcloth to the head of the lake are Great Gable and the Scafell range, an unforgettable panorama of colour and rock formation. The return journey to Ambleside can be made through Santon Bridge and Eskdale Green, where there is an Outward Bound Rescue School, to the foot of the Hardknott Pass. Alternatively, the A595 may be joined at Gosforth.

The screes across Wast Water

Tour 6   Ambleside, Rydal, Grasmere and Keswick

Take the A591 north from the town over Crow How to **Rydal Water,** a
small but delightful lake lying between the precipitous Nab Scar and
Loughrigg Fell. This is the first of the lakes to freeze in winter, making
it popular with skaters. The tiny hamlet of **Rydal** has rich associations
with William Wordsworth and the lake poets. **Rydal Mount,** where he
died in 1850 and in which he spent half his life, is open to the public
from April 1st to December 31st daily (except Mondays). Many personal
items and pieces of furniture used by the family are on display. The
church of St Mary, built in 1824, has a number of interesting windows,
including one dedicated to Thomas Arnold, Headmaster of Rugby
School. Through the churchyard is the field Wordsworth gave to his
daughter, now known as Dora's field, and owned by the National
Trust; in spring it is carpeted with daffodils. Rydal Park, a short
distance from the road, is the venue for the Vale of Rydal Sheepdog
Trials held on the second Thursday in August. In addition to the trials,
which include 'brace' competitions (two dogs working together), which
originated here in 1901, there is a show of working terriers, hounds and
beagles. This popular event draws competitors and spectators from far
afield. Approximately half way along the lake's northern shore stands
Nab Cottage, with the date 1702 above the door. It was here that
Hartley Coleridge spent the last eleven years of his life.

The road now leaves Rydal Water, but within 1½ km (1 ml) is hugging
the east shore of **Grasmere,** another small lake whose reeded shallows
are dominated by Helm Fell. The village offers places of interest, easy
walks and unique events and caters for visitors with gift shops and
artists studios. Standing amidst tall trees, the whitewashed **Dove
Cottage** was the home of Wordsworth for many years. The simple
furniture and stone-flagged floors remain. The walls are hung with
an interesting collection of portraits. When Wordsworth moved to
Allan Bank in 1808, Thomas de Quincey took over the tenancy and
lived at the cottage for the next 26 years. It is open to the public on
weekdays from April 1st to 30th September, 10 am–1 pm and 2–6 pm;
from 1st October to mid-January the cottage closes at 4.30 pm. On the
opposite side of the road, the **Wordsworth Museum,** housed in a
reconstructed barn, displays a typical 18th-century Lakeland kitchen
and many items, including manuscripts and first editions, belonging
to the poet. Open from Easter to 31st October as for Dove Cottage. The
museum is closed during the winter. The church of St Oswald has some
interesting stained glass windows and a poor box dated 1649 and is the
setting for the annual Rushbearing Ceremony which takes place on the
Saturday nearest to the 5th August (see page 34). Children are
traditionally rewarded with a piece of gingerbread, baked and sold
from the 'Old Cottage'; built in 1660 as the village school it was
converted to its present use in 1854. In the churchyard, by the banks of
the River Rothay, are the graves of William and Mary Wordsworth and
their family, also Hartley Coleridge and Sir John Richardson, the
famous Arctic explorer. The yew trees were planted by Wordsworth in
1819. Grasmere Sports, the Highland Games of the Lakes, take place
on the Thursday nearest 20th August and date back to 1868 when they

were founded to promote traditional Lakeland sports (see page 34).

An unclassified road leads from the village to **Loughrigg Terrace,** a gentle walk with a superb view. Travelling northwards, the A591 climbs steeply out of the Rothay Valley towards Dunmail Rise, with Fairfield, Dollywaggon Pike and Helvellyn towering majestically to the east. At the head of the pass is a large cairn, said to be the grave of Dunmail, the last king of Cumbria, whose defeat in battle at this spot in AD 945 brought Cumberland under Scottish rule for over a hundred years. Nowadays, this district is popular with climbers and with skiers during the winter. The road now descends to **Thirlmere,** a large lake converted to a reservoir in 1879 by Manchester Corporation. Water is supplied to the city by means of an aqueduct almost 160 km- (100 ml) long. Thickly planted pine woods enclose the lake and tend to restrict the views. The fast main road follows the eastern shore under the Helvellyn screes, but an unclassified road along the western side offers a more peaceful alternative; here rivers and gills tumble into the lake with falls at Launchy Gill and Dab Gill. There is no public access to the lake. After crossing St John's Beck, the two roads re-join, turning north west for **Keswick** a distance of about 8 km (5 ml).

Tour 7 Ambleside, Ullswater and Keswick

Follow Tour 1 to Holehird and proceed northwards to Troutbeck Bridge and **Troutbeck.** The road climbs steadily through magnificent scenery following the course of Trout Beck until it reaches the solitary Kirkstone Inn, the fifth highest licenced house in England. This is the beginning of the pass, the summit at 454 m (1489 ft) marked by the Kirk Stone after which it is named. Continuing through the rugged and towering heights of Raven Crag and Middle Dod to the west, and precipitous ranges of Caudale Moor to the east, the road drops down to **Brothers Water** in beautiful **Dovedale.** Goldrill Beck is followed to **Patterdale** village at the foot of Ullswater. This small village, lying in the vale of the same name, is famous for its connections with St Patrick. The church, built in 1853 and dedicated to the saint, has a curious clocktower in the north-east corner. The high ceiling is painted with stars, reminiscent of that in Carlisle Cathedral. St Patrick's well is unmarked and lies to the north of the village just beyond the point where Grisedale Beck enters the lake.

Ullswater, 11 km (7 ml) in length, is second in size only to Windermere and forms a dog leg round the fells of Martindale Common to the east and under the watchful eye of Helvellyn to the west. Reaching to a depth of 60 m (200 ft) the lake is only 1½ km (1 ml) across at the widest point. The road continues to **Glenridding,** an old mining village on the shore, now the terminus for motor yachts which cruise the lake. Boats may also be hired and private craft launched from here. From the village, a lane climbs steeply for 3 km (2 ml) to the disused lead mine of **Greenside.** Nearby is a climbing hut and mountain rescue post. The tour continues to **Glencoyne Park** (National Trust) and passes the junction of the A5091 for the A66 Keswick to Penrith road. In **Gowbarrow Park** (also National Trust) just before reaching Aira Beck, there is a large car-park for those wishing to follow the

series of footpaths and bridges round **Aira Force.** The waterfall, over
18 m (60 ft) high, cascades down a deep, winding ravine approximately
1 km ($\frac{1}{2}$ ml) from the road. The path to the higher fall, High Force, is
rather rough and can be slippery, calling for sturdy shoes. Lyulph's
Tower, a hunting lodge built by the Duke of Norfolk in 1780, stands
within private grounds and can be seen from the road. **Gowbarrow
Hall** is an outward bound school and mountain rescue post. The road
along the shore, with stopping places and view points, passes through
Watermillock to **Pooley Bridge,** where the River Eamont enters the
lake. This is the starting point for lake steamers which call at Howtown
and Glenridding. From here the visitor has a choice of roads;
i. An unclassified road down the eastern shore of Ullswater (no exit)
beneath Barton Fell to **Howtown** where there is a steamer pier and
the only public launching site for power-driven craft on the lake.
Ascend the steep Harlin Fell to visit the hamlet of **Martindale** and see
the tiny dale chapel of St Martin, built in 1633 with stone walls and
containing much Jacobean work. In the surrounding fells, the last herd
of wild red deer in England may be seen.

ii. The B5320 to Penrith, passes through **Yanwath** and **Eamont
Bridge,** and a detour southwards on unclassified roads leads to
Askham and Bampton before traversing the east side of **Haweswater**
Reservoir. Built in 1937 to supply water to Manchester, the lake lies
between Bampton Common and Swindale Common with the magnificent
High Street range at the southern end.

iii. Leaving Pooley Bridge by the A592, in 3 km (2 ml) an unclassified
road to the west leads to **Dacre,** a village which has much of interest
to offer visitors. The castle, by Dacre Beck, is a 14th-century pele
tower built as refuge against border raiders, and the home of the Lords
of Dacre for 300 years. Tastefully modernized, the castle contains many
fine tapestries and examples of period furniture from all over the
world. Open to the public, the castle may be viewed by appointment.
St Andrew's Church combines Norman and 14th-century work with
tiny, 13th-century lancet windows. Nearby **Hutton John** is a
14th-century pele tower with impressive Tudor additions including a
finely carved staircase. Not open to the public.

Crossing the A66 Keswick to Penrith road, a short detour on
unclassified roads may be made to **Greystoke,** a charming village set
round a green. The castle is in private ownership and not open to the
public, but the large church, dedicated to St Andrew is well worth
visiting.

Tourists may continue to either Penrith or Keswick on the A66, or
re-join the tour via the A5091 at Glencoyne Park for the return to
Ambleside.

Keswick is an interesting market town and one of the most popular
touring centres, standing at the head of Derwent Water, beneath the
towering slopes of Skiddaw. The A66, A591 and B5289 give access to all
parts of Lakeland, and outstanding viewpoints at Castlerigg and
Latrigg are within easy walking distance. At **Castlerigg,** a stone circle
$30\frac{1}{2}$ m (100 ft) in diameter and dating from 1400 BC is composed of 38

rough, unhewn stones which encompass an oblong of 10 stones. Now the property of the National Trust, access is unrestricted. In the market square, the black and white Moot Hall houses an Information Centre during the summer and is the starting point for guided walks. The **Fitz Park Trust Art Gallery and Museum** in Station Road houses a collection of birds native to the district, specimens of local minerals and stone axes from Langdale. The art gallery displays paintings by Nash and Turner, and original manuscripts and first editions by many of the Lakeland poets and writers. Open from Easter to the end of October, and during the winter months by appointment only. The **Pencil Museum,** in addition to explaining production techniques, also shows examples of fine art work. Open from May to September, 9 am–12.30 pm and 1.30–5.30 pm. Another unusual museum, the **Model Railway Exhibition** at the Railway Station, has almost 305 m (1000 ft) of track running through realistic settings, and is a must for all model railway enthusiasts. Open daily, except Sundays, from Easter to mid-October. Craft centres within the town display paintings, items made from Lakeland green stone, metalwork, sculpture, stoneware and pottery by local craftsmen and artists.

By the side of the Greta Bridge lies the footpath to **Portinscale,** 2½ km (1½ ml), a tiny village on the shore of the lake and a stopping place for lake steamers. There are boats for hire and at the headquarters of the Derwent Sailing Club visitors may launch dinghies on payment of a fee to the secretary at the clubhouse. The club holds mixed handicap racing from April to mid-October on alternate weekends. 1½ km (1 ml) from Portinscale on the western shore of the lake, **Lingholm Gardens** are open to the public daily except Sundays, from April to October. The gardens afford magnificent views and are noted for their flowering shrubs.

From the centre of Keswick, Lake Road provides a pleasant walk to the shores of **Derwent Water** where there are boat landings. A stone memorial to John Ruskin stands at Friars Crag, and from here the beauty of the lake may be fully appreciated, its surface dotted with wooded islands and lying beneath the steeply wooded slopes of Catbells, Brandlehow and Grange Fell. St Herbert's Island, accessible by boat, was the retreat of St Herbert in AD 685. A steamer sails the lake from Good Friday to mid-October (weather permitting) and calls at Ashness Landing (Ashness Bridge and Watendlath); Lodore Landing (waterfalls and High Brandlehow); Low Brandlehow (wooded picnic spots) and Hawse End Landing (Newlands Valley and Buttermere). Further details may be obtained from the Keswick and Derwentwater Launch Co. Ltd, 29 Manor Park, Keswick.

The lovely village of Troutbeck

Tour 8   Keswick, the Whinlatter Pass and Ennerdale

From Keswick take the A66 west, then the B5292 over the
Whinlatter Pass which was extensively planted in the 19th century, to
Lorton, Tour 10. Cross the Vale of Lorton to join the B5289 south to
the junction with the unclassified road, signposted **Loweswater.** The
small village stands slightly apart from the lake, which has footpaths
along the western shore to Helme Wood, owned by the National Trust,
with good views across to Darling Fell. The road passes beneath the
slopes of the fell, leaves the lake, and at Fangs Farm divides into two.
The lane to the west leads to Mockerkin and **Mockerkin Tarn,** set in
rolling meadows, the marshy ground providing a natural breeding
ground for curlews and ducks. Join the A5086 for Cockermouth, 10½ km
(6½ ml).

The second road turns south to Lamplugh, skirting Murton Fell
before reaching Croasdale Beck where it forks for Ennerdale Bridge
and **Ennerdale Water.** This remote lake lies at the beginning of a
narrow valley whose thickly wooded slopes are dwarfed by the mighty
peaks of Steeple, Pillar and Great Fell. The lane ends at Mireside and
footpaths continue along the northern shore through Latterbarrow and
Gillerthwaite in **Ennerdale Forest.** Beyond the lake is a mountain
rescue post and a climbing hut; from this point it is possible to climb
over Black Sail Pass to **Wast Water** or northwards through Scarth
Gap Pass to **Buttermere.** Returning to Ennerdale Bridge, a series of
unclassified roads lead to the A5086, **Egremont** and the coast.

Tour 9   Keswick, Bassenthwaite and Caldbeck

Leave the town on the A66 north to **Crosthwaite.** It was from here in a
clearing marked with a cross (from which the town took its name) that
St Kentigern, also known as St Mungo and adopted as Cumbria's own
saint, preached to the people in the 6th century. As his ministry spread
across Northern Lakeland, dedications were made in his name, notably
at Caldbeck, Castle Sowerby, Mungrisdale and **Bromfield** where the
well is enclosed by a sunken building known as St Mungo's Castle.
At Crosthwaite, the holy well he used for the baptism of his converts
can be seen in the churchyard. Fragments of the 12th-century
foundation are to be found in the 16th-century building, when
extensive alterations and additions were made. Of especial note are the
unique consecration crosses from this period, the Radcliffe brasses and
the white marble memorial to Robert Southey, Poet Laureate, with an
epitaph composed by William Wordsworth.

Take the A591, following the Derwent river valley to **Bassenthwaite**
Lake beneath the towering slopes of Skiddaw. This large lake, 6½ km
(4 ml) long, enjoys a peaceful atmosphere and boats may be hired from
Peelwyke boat landings. Arrangements may be made to launch sailing
dinghies from Bassenthwaite Sailing Club on payment of a small fee
(powered craft are not allowed). A sailing week in August attracts
visitors from far afield. A short distance from the main road, near the
head of the lake, is the village of Bassenthwaite, a cluster of grey
cottages beside Chapel Beck. There are two churches, St John's by
the road, the other dedicated to St Bega lies by the lake shore, reached

by footpaths from Dyke Nook about 3 km (2 ml) south of the village. The little Norman church with a crooked chancel and an ancient lead crucifix above the pulpit is well worth visiting. It was at this spot that Alfred, Lord Tennyson wrote *Mort d'Arthur*. At Castle Inn beyond the village, turn east on to an unclassified road to Uldale by the River Ellen, and northwards past the mill to **Ireby,** an attractive stone-built village with an old market cross and an interesting moot hall. At nearby **Ruthwaite, John Peel** was born in 1777. He spent most of his life in Caldbeck returning just before his death in 1854. Numerous relics including his crop, horn, a pair of stirrups and a bit may be seen in the Sun Garage, with a certificate of authenticity signed by two of his daughters. Join the B5299 westwards for **Caldbeck,** a scattered village with houses dating from 1666, it is renowned for its association with John Peel. A tall, hard-drinking, uncouth farmer with a great affinity for his hounds and horses, he lived for hunting, to the detriment of his family. Notoriety was achieved through the song *D'ye Ken John Peel* written on a winter's night in the Odd Fellows Arms by his great friend Robert Woodcock Graves, a worker at the woollen mill near the Howk where the 'cloth so grey' was made. Although he died at Ruthwaite, Peel is buried in the churchyard of St Kentigern's, the grave marked by a tall white stone to the left of the main path. Nearby is the grave of Mary of Buttermere whose story is told on page 70. Through the churchyard, by the stream, the remains of St Mungo's well can be found. The ancient church contains a wall behind the choir dating from 1118 and a small 13th-century leper window. At the south corner of the green, a path, rather overgrown and slippery, leads to the **Howk**—a spectacular limestone gorge with gigantic swallow holes; when the river is in spate one of these, called the Fairy Kettle, has the appearance of boiling water. Below the Howk stands the abandoned woollen mill where Peel's Iveson Grey cloth was made and, further up, a disused bobbin mill.

Returning to the B5299, travel west through tiny hamlets to the junction of the A595 at **Mealsgate.** George Moore, a philanthropist was born here and lived at **Whitehall,** the manor house. The pele tower was built in 1399, three stories high with embattled parapets, a two-storied extension was added some time later. Open by written appointment with Mrs S. Parker-Moore, 5 Eaton Villas, Chalk Farm, London NW3 4SX. All Hallow's Church is reached by a path near the house and contains memorials to George Moore and his family. Following the A595 south west to Bothel turn on to the A591 towards Bassenthwaite. At the hamlet of Bewaldeth, a detour to **Isel** by the River Derwent may be made. The small Norman church of St Michael stands in a delightful setting and has many interesting relics including an ancient gravestone and a unique stone thought to date back as far as the 5th century bearing a rare three-armed symbol called the triskele. There are also many memorials to local families. Across the fields at **Isel Hall,** a pele tower has been incorporated into a 16th-century mansion with fine mullioned windows. The hall is not open to the public. Returning to the A591, continue to Castle Inn at the junction with the B2591; standing in extensive grounds, **Armathwaite**

Hall, at the head of the lake, is now a hotel. Continue to the A66 crossing the Ouse Bridge, the road closely follows the west shore of Bassenthwaite Lake and affords fine views across the water to Dodd Wood and Skiddaw. Pass through Wythop Woods and Thornthwaite Forest to Braithwaite at the foot of the Whinlatter Pass and back to Portinscale and Keswick.

Tour 10   Keswick, Borrowdale, Honister Pass, Crummock Water and Vale of Lorton

From Keswick, the B5289 follows the eastern shore of Derwent Water to Barrow Bay, where an unclassified road (no exit) branches to the south east to Ashness Bridge and **Watendlath.** The old pack-horse bridge, one of the most photographed attractions in Lakeland, spans a stream that rushes down from Ashness Fell. Continue to Lodore, where Watendlath Beck enters the lake, a calling place for lake steamers and from where boats may be hired. From behind the hotel, the famous **Lodore Falls** may be seen, especially imposing after heavy rain, the 45 m- (150 ft) cascade squeezed between the crags. Follow the Derwent Valley to the village of **Grange-in-Borrowdale,** where the double-arched bridge over the river is a great favourite with artists. Lakeland Rural Industries Craft Centre, with showrooms and workshop, displays excellent examples of local crafts, and is open daily except Sundays. To the west of the village, Peace How was given by Canon Rawnsley as a war memorial, and is now owned by the National Trust. Grange and the surrounding countryside featured in many of the Herries stories written by Sir Hugh Walpole. This narrow and densely wooded point between Grange Fell and Lowscawdel is known as 'The Jaws of Borrowdale'. In a clearing to the east of the road, beneath the towering crags, is the **Bowder Stone,** an immense 2032 t (2000 ton) boulder, 10 m (35 ft) high, balanced on a knife edge, and which may be climbed by way of a ladder. Approaching Rosthwaite, the valley widens and the steep, green fells give way to craggy peaks as the road climbs sharply towards Seatoller. An unclassified road follows the river to **Seathwaite,** the wettest inhabited place in England, where Sourmilk Gill cascades into the Derwent. From here climbers begin their ascent of some of Lakeland's most famous peaks, Great Gable, Bow Fell, Pillar and Scafell. A mountain rescue post and climbing hut are situated at the end of the track.

Beyond Seatoller, the road continues to rise through gradients of 1 in 4, or steeper, with fine views over Borrowdale to the **Honister Pass,** 358 m (1176 ft), surrounded by wild, rugged scenery and overshadowed by Honister Crag, its flanks scarred by slate quarries. Following the course of Gatesgarth Beck, the way now passes through

*Packhorse bridge and Herdwick sheep, Wastdalehead
Grange-in-Borrowdale, bottom*

a deep fissure among the rocks, affording breathtaking views of the valleys and lakes below, before dropping down through Gatesgarth to **Buttermere.** This tiny lake, only 2 km (1¼ ml) in length, has wooded shores of pine and larch which quickly give way to the precipitous fells of Red Pike and High Stile, with the magnificent Fleetwith Pike at the head of the valley. At the northern end of the lake, the village of Buttermere stands on a level strath between the lake and **Crummock Water** at the foot of Newlands Hause. Footpaths lead from the village to the foot of Buttermere where Sourmilk Gill spills from tiny Bleaberry Tarn down waterfalls into the lake. Crossing the River Cocker which joins the two lakes, follow the path for a further 3 km (2 ml) to see the spectacular **Scale Force** where the beck drops 136 m (120 ft) in a single leap; one of the highest falls in England. In the village, a small church dated 1840 stands by the roadside. Dedicated to St James, it has an interesting east window and the sanctuary is paved with Honister slate. The Fish Hotel, set back from the road, features in a Lakeland legend, for it was here that **Mary of Buttermere** lived, and gained fame when she married James Hadfield in 1802; an imposter who had previously been married twice. After leaving both wives penniless, he came to Keswick, masquerading as a Member of Parliament. Although courting a rich lady there, he came to see the 'Beauty of Buttermere', and soon he and Mary were married in Lorton Church. James was finally arrested, not for bigamy, but forgery, and was executed at Carlisle in 1803. Mary gained much sympathy and became the heroine of many ballads and plays. She later married a farmer and is buried in Caldbeck Church.

An unclassified road leads from Buttermere north east over Newlands Hause and down Newlands Valley to Keswick. The B5289 follows the eastern shore of Crummock Water beneath Grasmoor Fells, from the small promontory viewpoint at **Hause Point,** extensive views may be enjoyed. Continuing northwards, leave the lake and pass through the Vale of Lorton to **Low Lorton** described in Tour 8. **Lorton Hall,** open on Bank Holidays and at other times by appointment with the owner, the Rev. J. A. Woodhead-Keith-Dixon, has been the home of the Winder and Dixon families since before the Norman Conquest. The original pele tower dates from 1050 and was visited by King Malcolm III and Queen Margaret of Scotland in 1089. A medieval range of domestic quarters was built on to the later 15th-century tower. The chapel, re-consecrated in 1965, marks the spot where monks, carrying the body of St Cuthbert, rested in AD 850. The house contains beautiful oak panelling, and Jacobean and Carolean furniture. Between the villages of High and Low Lorton is the church, also dedicated to St Cuthbert, dated 1887 and standing on the site of an earlier building. In the churchyard there are some interesting tombstones. Behind the village hall is the famous yew tree where George Fox, the Quaker, preached.

The tourist may now join the B5292 turning east, over the Lorton Fells, Whinlatter Pass and Portinscale to Keswick; or north west to Cockermouth, Tour 9, the A594 and A595 coast roads or north east to Carlisle, 42 km (26 ml).

GAZETTEER

ABBEY TOWN Renowned for the great **Holm Cultram Abbey,** it is situated on the River Waver at the south-east corner of Moricambe Bay. The abbey was founded in 1150 by monks from the Cistercian Abbey at Melrose, and became one of the largest monastic houses in the North of England. The target for marauding Scots, it was mercilessly sacked and stripped of its wealth. After the Dissolution in 1538, the building became a quarry of stone for the new farming community. The abbey has continued to serve as the parish church and has regained importance as an arts centre. A festival held in June is becoming internationally famous, and throughout the year some 200 other events take place.

The surrounding area, although flat, is designated as being of outstanding beauty. The villages of Allonby and Bowness on the coast and those of Kirkbride and West Newton inland, possess a charm which delights the visitor. At Wigton, the market town, there are several buildings of interest. *Information Centre—Holm Cultram Abbey, will supply details of the Arts Centre and the surrounding countryside. Tel. Abbey Town 654.*

AMBLESIDE (pop. 2657) An attractive tourist centre at the intersection of the A591 and A593, is the starting point for tours of Southern Lakeland, nos. 1–7. Within easy reach of Windermere town and all the amenities of the lake as well as Coniston, Rydal and Grasmere. The nearest coastal resort is Grange-over-Sands, 42 km (26 ml). The pretty Bridge House, over Stock Ghyll, is now the Information Centre of the National Trust. St Mary's Church, designed by Sir Gilbert Scott, is the setting for the annual Rushbearing Ceremony. Waterhead Pier serves the Sealink cruisers and as a landing stage for hired and private boats. The gardens at **White Craggs, Stagshaw** and those of the Lakeland Horticultural Society at the Leonard Cheshire Home at **Holehird,** are open daily throughout the year, and are exceptionally beautiful at springtime. Watersports and outdoor activities are catered for.

All types of accommodation are available, from luxury hotels to camping and caravan sites and youth hostels. *National and local buses serve the area; Nearest station—Windermere; Early closing— Thursday; Information Offices—the Old Court House, Church Street. Tel. (096 63) 2582; National Park Information Centre. Tel. (096 63) 3084; National Trust, Bridge House; National Trust Regional Office, Broadlands, Borrans Road. Information on National Trust properties only. Tel. (096 63) 3003; Lake District National Park Mobile Unit, Waterhead car-park.*

APPLEBY (pop. 1855) Situated on the banks of the River Eden within easy reach of Lakeland to the west and the Pennines to the east, the town is served by the A66 Penrith to Barnard Castle road, and the B6260 to Kendal. The Moot Hall is one of many interesting old buildings in Boroughgate, the main street. At the foot of the hill, Low Cross, a tall 19th-century pillar, stands adjacent to the Cloisters, whilst at the summit an older pillar indicates the site of the town's earliest market. Nearby are the gates of the castle, now a private residence and not open to the public. This was one of the homes of Lady Anne Clifford who lies buried in the church of St Lawrence at the lower end of Boroughgate. The church was destroyed during the Scots raids in 1174, and rebuilt four years later by order of Henry II. St Michael's Church in Bongate has a Scandinavian hogback gravestone in the north wall.

Within easy touring distance are the beautiful Eden Valley, the extensive ruins of **Brough Castle,** and the scant remains of **Pendragon Castle,** Mallerstang, the reputed home of Uther Pendragon, father of King Arthur.

For leisure activities, the town offers angling, an 18-hole golf course, heated, open-air swimming pool and local pony trekking. There is hotel, guesthouse and self-catering accommodation and facilities for touring and motor caravans. *Early closing— Thursday; Market day—Saturday; Bus Services—Ribble Motor Services provide local transport, and a number of express coach services stop by arrangement; Appleby Railway Station is on the London Midland Region line from Carlisle to London; Tourist Information Centre—Betty's Corner, The Cloisters. Tel. (0930) 51659.*

ASKHAM (pop. 385) A small village situated by the River Lowther on an unclassified road 8 km (5 ml) south of Penrith, included in Tour 7 ii. **Askham Hall,** an Elizabethan mansion with a 14th-century pele tower is the home of the Earl of Lonsdale. The 5th earl was first president of the Automobile Association and originator of the 'Lonsdale Belt'. **Lowther Park** across the river has an interesting medieval church of St Michael, a monument to the Lowther family. The original 13th-century manor house was destroyed by fire in 1725 and rebuilt in 1811; this in turn was demolished leaving the shell seen today, 128 m (420 ft) long with symetric turrets and embattled towers. The Wild Life Park occupies over 40½ h (100 acres) and is described in full on page 31. Accommodation is limited—the Activity Centre offers self-catering facilities for groups and families. *On a limited bus route; Nearest station—Penrith.*

BARROW-IN-FURNESS (pop. 63,340) Renowned for shipbuilding, Barrow is à large industrial town on the southernmost point of the Furness Peninsula, on the A590 and A5087 (Tour 4). It was from here that the first schooner was launched in 1852. A small maritime museum is housed in the Central Library, Ramsden Street. Modern Barrow provides all the amenities expected from a town its size; facilities for watersports being found on the islands. Walney Island, 17½ km (11 ml) long, is connected to the mainland by a modern opening bridge and has one of the finest nature reserves in Cumbria (see page 31). The lighthouse is not open. On Piel Island, reached only by boat, the monks of Furness Abbey built a castle against sea invasion by the Scots—now in ruins. It was on the island that Lambert Simnel landed in 1487 in his bid for the throne. The long stretches of sandy beach on the peninsula's east coast afford excellent bathing. Hunting on foot with the North Lonsdale Fox Hounds is popular in winter.

To the north of the town is **Furness Abbey,** the finest monastic ruins in the country. In the care of the Department of the Environment, it is open on weekdays from 9.30 am–5.30 pm; November–February to 4 pm; May–September until 7 pm; Sundays open from 2 pm. Accommodation is limited. *Early closing—Thursday; Market days—Wednesday and Saturday; National and local buses serve the area; on British Rail main line from London, Euston; Information centre—Civic Halls, Duke Street. Tel. (0229) 25795.*

BEWCASTLE (pop. 335) On an unclassified road due north of the A69 Carlisle to Hexham road, this was an outpost for the Roman legions at Carlisle. Within its boundaries the fort contains the castle, church, rectory and a farm. The Anglo-Saxons, who appropriated the fort after the withdrawal of the garrison, erected the magnificent cross for which the village is famous. Established as 7th century, the 4 m- (14 ft) shaft is unique for its religious carvings, different on each face. North of the church are the remains of Bueth's Castle which was destroyed by Oliver Cromwell; the ancient church of St Cuthbert was, like the castle, built with stones from the Roman settlement in the 12th century, and is unusual as there are no windows on the north side. The Roman cauldron found at Bewcastle and a replica of the cross are to be seen in Tullie House Museum, Carlisle. *Nearest station—Carlisle.*

BRAMPTON (pop. 3895) An ancient town on the A69 from Carlisle overlooking the Irthing Valley, with much of interest to offer the visitor. St Martin's Church, late 19th century, contains glass designed by William Morris; nearby, the octagonal Moot Hall of 1817 has an outer staircase to an upper entrance. It was in the town that Prince Charles Edward Stewart received the keys of Carlisle in 1745. Protected to the east by a motte of exceptional height, the town was well fortified against border raids.

North west on an unclassified road is **Lanercost Abbey,** the original nave is in continual use as the parish church, a wall dividing the east end from the extensive abbey ruins (see page 13). In the care of the Department of the Environment, it is open at standard hours. From Banks, the road closely follows the line of the **Roman Wall** to Gilsland and the Northumbrian border. Various milecastles and forts are to be found in the area and are open to the public at any reasonable times. At **Over Denton** the old church was constructed with stones from the Roman Wall and it has an original Roman chancel arch, of which there are only two in the country. The ruined barn was a pele tower and is known as 'The Vicarage'. **Nawarth Castle,** south of the river is the 14th-century home of the Earl of Carlisle. Greatly added to in the 16th and 17th centuries, it was badly damaged by fire in 1844 and re-created by Salvin in the old style. Lord William's Tower contains a magnificent timber ceiling removed from Kirkoswald

73

Castle. The richly panelled great hall is the largest in the country. Open for organized parties on application to the Earl of Carlisle at the castle.

Hotel and farmhouse accommodation is available, together with a touring caravan site. *Local bus service; Nearest station—Carlisle; Information Office—the Post Office, Front Street. Tel. Brampton 2301.*

BROUGHTON-IN-FURNESS An attractive village at the junction of the A593 and A595. The square, surrounded by chestnut trees, has an ancient fish slab, stocks and an obelisk in memory of John Gilpin. The church of St Mary stands on the site of a much earlier building and retains a fine Norman doorway on the south side. The dungeons and a tower are all that remain of the castle, now a school, although several footpaths lead through the grounds. Broughton is a good centre from which to tour the Duddon Valley (Tour 3); the Furness Peninsula, Millom and the west coast (Tour 4).

Hotels, guesthouses and farms offer accommodation and there is a site for touring caravans. *Market day—Thursday; On a main bus route; Nearest station—Foxfield, with a limited service from Barrow.*

BUTTERMERE (pop. 110) A tiny village standing between two lakes, Buttermere and Crummock Water, at the foot of Newlands Hause. The B5289 Keswick to Cockermouth road passes through the village (see Tour 10) and an unclassified road leads through the Newlands Valley to Keswick. There are footpaths to nearby waterfalls at Sourmilk Gill and Scale Force, one of the highest falls in the country with a single leap of 36½ m (120 ft). The Fish Hotel has connections with the legendary Mary of Buttermere who gained fame after her marriage to the imposter James Hadfield. The wayside church dated 1840 is dedicated to St James. There is good fishing in the vicinity, and excellent opportunities for rock climbing, mountaineering and fell walking. The walking centre at Hassness is nearby.

There is very limited hotel accommodation. *A rural mini-bus service operates from Easter to October daily from Keswick to Buttermere via the Newlands Pass, and Monday to Friday via the Whinlatter Pass. Details from Davies of Keswick, 23 Helvellyn Street, Keswick. Tel. (0596) 72676.*

CALDBECK (pop. 630) Famous for its connections with John Peel, this interesting village has much to offer the visitor (see Tour 9). The church is dedicated to St Kentigern, and in the churchyard the tall, white gravestone of John Peel will be found to the left of the path. Mary of Buttermere is also buried here; her story is told on page 70. Through the churchyard are the remains of St Mungo's Well. The Howk is a spectacular limestone gorge with gigantic swallow holes.

Of interest nearby are Hesket Newmarket, where the hall has a circular roof and twelve angled walls (not open to the public); and Mungrisdale, a tiny hamlet of whitewashed cottages, where the spectre army of Soutar Fell was seen for the first time in 1735. In 1745 the villagers swore an affidavit after watching vast legions march over the fells for an hour before disappearing over a precipice.

Caldbeck lies within excellent fell-walking country, and the neighbouring village of Threlkeld is the main centre for climbing Blencathra, or Back o' Skidda as it is sometimes called, where John Peel hunted with his hounds.

Road connections are provided by the B5299 from Carlisle to Mealsgate and the A595. There is very limited accommodation available locally.

CARK-IN-CARTMEL An attractive hamlet overlooking Ulverston Sands. **Cark Hall,** not open to the public, is a late 16th-century house with tiny mullioned windows, where the Quaker, George Fox, was held prisoner. Close by, **Holker Hall** on the B5278, is the late 16th-century home of the Cavendish family. The new wing, rebuilt in 1871 after a disastrous fire, is open to the public. The exquisite woodcarving is a feature of the house, which was entirely constructed of local stone and timber from the estate. Treasures collected over the centuries by the Dukes of Devonshire include furniture, silver and paintings. Open daily, except Saturday, from Easter Sunday to 30th September from 10.30 am–6 pm. Additional facilities include a deer park with four species of deer, children's play area, craft centre, gift shop and café. On Sundays, weather permitting, a hot air balloon can be seen in flight. The Lakeland Rose Show is staged in the park annually in July.

The nearest town is Grange-over-Sands, 8 km (5 ml) where there are sports facilities and excellent accommodation of all categories. The village lies on the B5277 from Grange to Haverthwaite and the A590. *It is on the Carlisle to Carnforth coastal railway route; Local bus services are provided by the Ribble Motor Services Ltd, Grange. Tel. (044 84) 2208.*

CARLISLE (pop. 69,865) The county town of Cumbria is situated in the north of the region with excellent communications to Glasgow and London. Scene of many battles in which it has changed hands innumerable times, the last being only 200 years ago during the 1745 Jacobite Rebellion. The city's history can be traced through the old walls and buildings. Emperor Hadrian built his 117 km-(73 ml) long wall through here in AD 122. Starting from Bowness-on-Solway, small forts or milecastles were erected at mile intervals, each with two turrets between. The width of the wall varied between $2\frac{1}{2}$ m–3 m (8–10 ft). Within the Cumbrian border a number of large forts were built, the largest being at Carlisle with a garrison for 1000 men. (Others were established at Stanwix, Burgh-by-Sands and Castleheads.) At **Tullie House Museum,** a remarkably comprehensive collection of Roman antiquities are displayed, and excavations in the grounds show fragments of the ancient city. Henry I founded an Augustinian priory in 1122, and by 1133 had created the See of Carlisle. The **cathedral,** containing much Norman work, and the priory buildings are described on page 13. Much of the old town is contained within a comparatively small area and can easily be explored on foot. Outside the station, the visitor is greeted by the twin towers of the **Citadel,** the original southern gateway; restored in 1807, it now houses the Crown Court. Opposite, a road leads to **Market Place,** with a cross erected in 1682 marking the Roman city centre, and from where Prince Charles Stewart proclaimed his father to be James III. Annually on 26th August, Carlisle Great Fair is announced from the steps. **St Cuthbert's Church,** founded by the saint in AD 685 was re-built in 1778 and contains the mayoral pew and a unique, movable pulpit. St Cuthbert founded many churches throughout Cumbria at this time, his journeys taking him down as far as Cartmel, where he was granted land 'with all the Britons in it'. Dedications made in the 8th century followed the path of the monks of Lindisfarne who carried his body in flight from the Danes. Wherever the cortège rested, a cross was erected to mark the spot. In the churchyard is a 15th-century tythe barn, unusual for being within the city walls. It is possible to walk parts of the walls from here to the Deanery in the cathedral precincts. Standing on high ground overlooking the River Eden is the **castle,** divided from the town by two ditches. The complete Norman keep is evidence of the castle's strength, which was increased by successive Scottish and English kings. Since 1702 it has been the 'home' of the Border Regiment, and their museum is housed in Queen Mary Tower.

South west of the city on the B6253 is the village of **Wetheral.** Of the priory, founded in 1100 for monks of the Benedictine Order, nothing remains except the ruined 15th-century gatehouse; now part of a farm, it can be clearly seen from the churchyard. Holy Trinity Church suffered much pillaging and destruction in border raids, but contains relics from the 13th century onwards. There is an interesting walk along the banks of the River Eden to Wetheral Caves. Cut into the rock, they are traditionally associated with St Constantine, and known to be at least 600 years old. On the opposite bank, a statue of the saint has been erected. Across the river, spanned by an imposing viaduct built in 1830, stands **Corby Castle.** The oldest part of the present house is 14th century and incorporates an even older pele tower. Acquired by Sir William Howard in 1611, the property was enlarged and altered in the 17th century and again in 1809. Tours can be arranged by prior appointment with Mrs John Howard at the castle. The gardens are open on Thursday, Saturday and Sunday from 2–7 pm. By rejoining the A69, tours can be taken to include Brampton, Gilsland, Bewcastle and many of the stations of **Hadrian's Wall.**

Modern Carlisle provides a compact shopping area, evening entertainment and sporting facilities. Boating is available on a small lake in the park beside the river. There are three golf courses in the vicinity, an athletics track, dry-ski slope and, to the south of the town, the well-situated race course.

Accommodation is provided in hotels, guesthouses and inns, two motels and in the surrounds, camping and caravan sites. There is also a youth hostel. *Early closing— Thursday; Market days— Wednesday and Saturday; National and local buses serve the area; Carlisle is a British Rail Inter-city and Motorail terminal, and has fast connections to London and Glasgow; Information Centre—M6 service area, Southwaite; and Old Town Hall. Tel. (0228) 25517 and 25396.*
CARTMEL Situated 3 km (2 ml) west of Grange-over-Sands on an unclassified road, Cartmel is dominated by the ancient priory church, founded in 1188 (see page 14). Part of the monastic buildings, the Priory Gatehouse (National Trust), contains relics of old crafts and industries (a guide is on duty).

Open daily, except Sunday, Easter Saturday to the end of September, from 10 am–5 pm. In Cavendish Street is the Anvil Gallery and Helen Bradley Centre, exhibiting a wide variety of paintings by northern artists. Open throughout the year daily, except Sunday, from 10 am–5 pm: admission is free. Nearby, the 17th-century 'Old Smithy' is complete with period equipment: local handicrafts are also displayed. Open daily throughout the year, except Sunday, 9.30 am–5.30 pm. Wood sculptor Michael Gibbon has created a unique gallery in an ancient crook barn, possibly the only one in Cumbria. All the old timbers have been retained, and the barn, built in 1658, provides a perfect setting for the display of his work. Open all the year from 9.30 am–7 pm, May to the end of October: November to the end of April closing at 4.30 pm. Mr Gibbon will open at other times on request to him at the house.

Spring and Summer Bank Holidays attract large crowds to the steeplechase races. In the vicinity are the fishing hamlet of Flookburgh and **Holker Hall,** Cark-in-Cartmel.

CARTMEL FELL Reached by unclassified roads due south of Windermere, between the A5074 and A592, is this hamlet of a few grey-stone cottages and the ancient chapel of St Anthony. Mainly 16th century with low saddle-backed roof and mullioned windows, it is set on the side of the hill so that the floor slopes down to the altar, and contains much rare 15th and 16th-century work. In the vicinity are some fine examples of old farmhouses, especially **Hodge Hill** which has a spinning gallery. The surrounding gentle fells are ideal for picnics and walking and afford views to Morecambe Bay.

COCKERMOUTH (pop. 6420) An interesting old market town, famous as the birthplace of William Wordsworth, and an excellent touring centre for Northern Lakeland. Many good roads converge on the town, the A595 from Carlisle, the A594 from Maryport and the A66 Workington to Keswick road. The Cumbrian coast and the lakes of Bassenthwaite, Derwent Water, Buttermere, Crummock Water and Loweswater are all within easy reach (see Tours 8 and 10). Wordsworth House in Main Street, now owned by the National Trust, is open to the public from Easter Saturday to the end of September, daily, except Fridays and Sundays. Two rooms may be visited, the dining room and the sitting room, where many of Wordsworth's books and possessions are on display. Memorials to the poet within the town include a stained-glass window in All Saints' Church, a fountain in Harris Park and a bronze head on a granite column at the junction of Gallowbarrow and Main Street.

The castle grounds are open at all reasonable times, and there are guided tours of the castle when Lord Egremont is not in residence. The original structure was possibly 12th century, but this was captured and destroyed by Robert the Bruce in 1315. The present building dates back to 1360, and although partly in ruins much of interest remains. Included in the guided tours are the secret dungeons or *oubliettes,* reached by trapdoors, and the Mirk Kirk, or dark chapel, founded about 1221.

In 1764, Fletcher Christian was born in Moorland Close, where the house still remains. He was later to gain fame for his part in the mutiny on the *Bounty*, and many links are still retained between Cockermouth and the Pitcairn Islands. The parish church of All Saints, built in 1854, stands on the site of two earlier churches. The tower, 54 m (180 ft) high, forms a distinctive landmark. In the churchyard is the grave of Wordsworth's father.

There is a golf course on the outskirts of the town, and anglers will find good fishing in the local rivers. There is motel, hotel and guesthouse accommodation, and many local inns and farmhouses provide bed and breakfast. A number of camping sites are situated within easy reach. *Early closing—Thursday; Market Day— Monday (the market charter was granted in 1222); Local buses are provided by the Cumberland Motor Services Ltd; Nearest station— Maryport; Tourist Information Office—Riverside, Market Street. Tel. (090 082) 2634 and 2376.*

CONISTON (pop. 1114) On the A593 and B5285 and included in Tours 1 and 4, is this busy village catering mainly for those visitors following outdoor pursuits. Narrow streets flanked by grey-stone cottages surround the church where John Ruskin is buried and the nearby museum bears his name. Across the lake, his house, Brantwood, now an art gallery and museum, is open to the public. Details of both museums can be found on page 23. A memorial to Sir Donald Campbell stands in the square, a reminder that it was on Coniston Water that he lost his life attempting the World Water Speed record in 1967. Coniston Old Man 801 m (2631 ft) overlooks the lake and is popular with walkers and rock climbers. Access to the lake is restricted, but the public may launch any type of craft from the camping sites along the shore or from the Coniston Boating Centre. During the winter months, the Coniston Fox Hounds meet and hunt within the area. Tarn Hows, 5 km (3 ml) north east is a popular beauty spot as is the Duddon Valley (Tour 3).

Accommodation is limited to guest and farmhouses, two youth hostels and camping sites. *Limited buses; Nearest station— Windermere via the ferry.*

DACRE (pop. 955) Lies between the A66 and A592, 7 km (4½ ml) from Penrith beside Dacre Beck. The castle, classified as an ancient monument, is a perfect example of a complete pele tower (view by appointment). St Andrew's Church, built on Saxon and Norman foundations, is mainly of the 14th century. The signing of the Peace of Dacre in 926 by the Kings of Cumberland, Scotland and England, is commemorated by the cross shaft to be found in the chancel. Within the area is the Elizabethan Manor of Hutton John and the charming village of Greystoke (Tour 7 iii). Nearby, Ullswater offers many tourist attractions combined with spectacular scenery (Tour 7).

DALTON (pop. 11,217) At the junction of the A590 and A595 (Tour 4) Dalton retains a massive pele tower from the 13th-century castle, built by the Abbot of Furness to protect the abbey from marauding Scots. Now a museum and housing an interesting collection of armour, it is owned by the National Trust. The key may be obtained from 18 Market Place and admission is free. In the churchyard of St Mary's is the grave of George Romney, born at Beckside, he returned to the area before his death in 1802. On Easter Sunday and Monday the ancient custom of Pace Egging takes place in the town. In the valley known as 'Beckonsgill' or 'Vale of the Deadly Nightshade', near Barrow, are the red-sandstone ruins of **Furness Abbey.** Ulverston, centre of the Furness area lies 6½ km (4 ml) north west. *Early closing— Wednesday; On Ribble bus route; On British Rail London Midland Region from Barrow.*

EAMONT BRIDGE and YANWATH (pop. 185) Two small villages lying to the south of Penrith, between the A66, A6 and B6262. The ancient river crossing marked the disputed Scottish border until 1237. There are a number of old houses, and perhaps most interesting of all, two ancient Henge monuments. **Arthur's Round Table** (1800 BC) comprises a flat area 91½ m (300 ft) in diameter surrounded by a dry moat. Here Charles II and his army camped on their way to Worcester. **Mayburgh** (2000 BC) has an embankment of cobbles and earth and a large single standing stone. It is unique among Henge monuments as it has no ditch. Both sites are under the care of the Department of the Environment. To the east of the village on the B6262, stands the parish church of Ninekirks at Brougham. In the 5th century, St Ninian, who was especially associated with the north west, formed a settlement on the banks of the River Eden and this became the foundation of the present church. In defiance of Cromwell in 1660, Lady Anne Clifford rebuilt the church and her initials 'A.P.' can be seen on the east wall, together with many memorials and brasses of the Brougham families. The Chapel of St Wilfred contains exquisite medieval carving and wall panels. The only form of illumination is provided by candlelight, giving the chapel a unique atmosphere. Almost completely destroyed during the Civil War, Brougham Castle was rebuilt by Lady Anne, but by 1714 after her death, was again in ruins. Portions still remain including the outer gatehouse, ground and first-floor rooms and the keep or Pagan Tower. The castle is now under the care of the Department of the Environment and is open to the public daily. Shortly after the B6262 joins the A66, will be seen the Countess Pillar, erected by Lady Anne to the memory of her mother.

The nearest town to Eamont Bridge is Penrith, approx. 2½ km (1½ ml) north, with excellent accommodation and sporting facilities. On the opposite side of the M6 motorway lies Yanwath, with one of the finest manorial halls in the country. Built in 1322, it incorporates a massive, square pele tower. Now forming part of the Lowther estate, the hall is not open to the public.

EGREMONT (pop. 7205) On the A595 and A5086 (Tour 7 ii) it is accessible from the Esk Valley (Tour 5) and the west-coast towns. Situated on the River Ehen it was, in Norman times, the capital of Copeland and here, in 1130, William de Meschine built his castle. The ruined gatehouse has some unusual rib vaulting and pleasing herringbone masonry, which can also be seen in the curtain wall. Parts of the 13th-century great hall block indicate the height of the building; traces of other domestic buildings can be seen. There is free access. Situated in the wide main street is the recently opened Lowes Court Gallery where exhibitions of paintings and local crafts are staged. Also the local Information Centre, it is open from Spring Bank Holiday to Christmas, on Tuesday, Thursday, Friday and Saturday 10 am–1 pm and 2–5 pm. Visitors who are in Lakeland during September should visit the Egremont Crab Fair, held annually since 1267 (see page 34). *Early closing—Wednesday; Market day—Friday; On Cumberland Bus Services route; On British Rail main line to Whitehaven; Tourist Information Centre—Lowes Court Gallery, Main Street. Tel. (094 682) 693.*

FLOOKBURGH The centre of the Morecambe Bay shrimp industry: fishermen still take a horse and cart on to the beach to gather in the harvest of flooks or flukes (small plaice), cockles and shrimps. An unusual weather-vane in the form of a fish surmounts the church where a charter granted by Edward I is kept.

The village lies on the B5277 from Grange to Haverthwaite and the A590. *Nearest town and station —Grange-over-Sands; Local bus services are provided by the Ribble Motor Services Ltd, Grange. Tel. (044 84) 2208.*

GOSFORTH (pop. 1020) Lies east of the A595 (Tour 5). The attractive stone houses, many with mullioned windows of 17th-century origin, present a pleasing picture. St Mary's Church incorporates much Norman work within its structure, the 10th century being represented by hogback tomb covers, and of greatest interest to visitors is the famous Gosforth Cross. Standing to a height of $4\frac{1}{2}$ m (15 ft), the shaft is believed to be the tallest in England; although well weathered,

the carvings can be easily traced. Near the centre of the churchyard is an old cork tree, the only one in Lakeland. Past the church, a lane leads to the villages of Wellington and Winnerath. From here it is possible to walk up to Sampsons Bratful Long Cairn. The cairn, so far unexcavated, measures 29 m (96 ft) long by $13\frac{1}{2}$ m (45 ft) at the widest part. Superb views are obtained towards the crags of Haycock, Steeple and Pillar. *On Cumberland Motor Services bus route; Nearest station—Seascale.*

GRANGE-IN-BORROWDALE A tiny village of distinct charm lying beyond the southern end of Derwent Water (see Tour 10). The double-arched bridge is a favourite with artists, and the surrounding countryside featured in many of Sir Hugh Walpole's stories. There are two chapels, one built of grey slate with an interesting barrel-shaped ceiling. Peace How was given as a war memorial by Canon Rawnsley, and is now National Trust property. The studios of Lakeland Rural Industries display examples of local craftwork and are open daily, except Sunday. The village stands on the B5289 within easy reach of Keswick.

GRANGE-OVER-SANDS (pop. 3500) Sheltered on three sides by wooded fells, Grange enjoys a mild climate, making this a popular holiday resort. The town is served by the B5272 and B5277 which run parallel from the A590 at Lindale. The mile-long, traffic-free promenade is safe for children, for whom the stretches of sand are a delight. Amenities for visitors include a shore-side swimming pool, two golf courses and local pony trekking. For those wishing to walk, Yewbarrow Crag and Hampsfell Hospice (where a shelter has been erected) offer fine views over the bay and to the north the mountains of Scafell, Skiddaw and Helvellyn. Ornithologists are catered for at the nature reserves of **Roundsea Wood** and **Rusland Moss** and permits can be obtained from Merlewood Research Station, Grange.

On certain Sundays during the summer months cross-bay walks are organized. It cannot be stressed too strongly that these should never be attempted alone. For further details contact the Official Guide to the Sands, Guides Farm, Cart Lane, Grange; or enquire at the Information Centre.

There is a wide range of accommodation from hotels and guesthouses to self-catering cottages, flats and caravan sites. Lakeland is within easy reach: Windermere is only 11 km (7 ml) away making this an excellent touring centre for both the lakes and coastline. *Early closing— Thursday (except during season); There are good local bus services to many nearby towns, including Kendal, Windermere, Cartmel and Ulverston. Details from Ribble Motor Services, Grange. Tel. (044 84) 2208; There are main line British Rail Inter-City and Sleeper services to Barrow and for London via Carnforth. Rover Runabout tickets are available on rail and steamer travel throughout the area; Information Centre—Council Offices, Main Street. Tel. (044 84) 2375. Services include Mountain Goat Booking Office and accommodation details. Open all year round, Monday–Friday 9 am– 5 pm.*

GRASMERE (pop. 990) Standing at the very centre of the Lake District National Park, this delightful village at the head of Grasmere enjoys an air of quiet tranquillity. Little has changed since Wordsworth made his home here at Dove Cottage (see Tour 6). The A591 Keswick to Ambleside road passes through the village, and an unclassified road leads south to Loughrigg Terrace. St Oswald's Church, where Wordsworth and many of his family are buried, is the setting for the annual Rushbearing Ceremony.. Grasmere Sports held in August (for details of both see page 34) are one of Lakeland's premier attractions. Also held in Grasmere are the Lake Artists Society Annual Exhibition (August and September) and an Antique Fair in October. Sporting facilities for the visitor include boating and fishing on the lake, and rock climbing— the Langdales, Great Gable, Scafell and Pillar are all within easy reach. There is excellent hotel, guesthouse and farmhouse accommodation, caravan sites nearby, and a youth hostel. *Early closing—Thursday; Brown's Motor Coach Tours, operating from ᵗAmbleside, pick up in the village and offer day and afternoon tours of Lakeland. Leaflet available from their office in Market Street, Ambleside, or locally from Beck Steps Sweetshop, Grasmere. Tel. (096 65) 475; Grasmere is a recognized stop on the Ribble Motor Service route from Keswick to Lancaster, providing connections to Ambleside, Windermere, Levens and Kendal; Nearest station— Windermere; Information Office— Broadgate News Agency, Grasmere. Tel. (096 65) 245.*

GREAT SALKELD (pop. 345) A charming village of red-sandstone houses, west of the River Eden. The church of St Cuthbert, overlooking the green, has an ancient foundation and one of the best-preserved pele towers in the area, dating from about 1380. Of special note is the beautiful south doorway with carving showing emblems of Scandinavian mythology. The villages of Great and Little Salkeld are divided by the River Eden, crossed at Langwathby or Lazonby. To the north of Little Salkeld stands **Long Meg and Her Daughters,** a circle of 59 stones 364 m (1200 ft) in circumference and second only in size to Stonehenge.

Sporting facilities in the area include excellent fishing in the River Eden and a heated, open-air swimming pool at Lazonby. The village stands on the B6412 which joins the A686 south for Penrith. *Local bus services are provided by Ribble Motor Services on their Penrith to Carlisle route. Details from their area office at Middlegate, Penrith. Tel. (0768) 3616.*

GREYSTOKE (pop. 520) A village grouped round a pleasant green, and lying on the B5288. There are some old, grey-stone houses, and on the green itself a tall, ancient cross. **Greystoke Castle,** built in 1353, was the home of the Howard family for 400 years. The grounds can be seen through an arched gateway, but neither the grounds nor the castle are open to the public. In a lane leading to the church will be seen the medieval sanctuary stone, now protected by an iron grille. The church of St Andrew was at one time a collegiate church with six chaplains. Dating from the 13th, 14th and 15th centuries the interior contains some old oak stalls and a magnificent east window.

The village is within easy reach of Ullswater and Northern Lakeland. *Bus connections are provided by Ribble Motor Services to Keswick and Penrith; Nearest town and station—Penrith; A mobile information unit at the Sportsman's Inn provides information for motoring tourists. Tel. Greystoke 492.*

HAWKSHEAD (pop. 633) A small and very popular village at the junction of the B5285 and B5286 from Ambleside and the Windermere ferry to Coniston (Tour 1). Visitors are advised to park their cars and explore the village on foot. Attractive courts and alleys are surrounded by pretty whitewashed cottages, much loved by Wordsworth when he was at school here. The ancient Courthouse contains an interesting museum of Lakeland Life (National Trust). Modern industry is displayed in the several craft shops. At **Satterthwaite,** the Grizedale Wild Life Centre offers opportunities for the naturalist with Photo-safari, aspects of forestry and deer preservation. The unique Theatre in the Forest is well worth visiting and advance booking is advised; details will be found on page 36. The home of Beatrix Potter is at **Near Sawrey,** at the foot of Esthwaite Water and many of her lovable characters can be imagined in the surrounding countryside. Tracks from Near Sawrey lead on to Claife Heights where extensive pine woods enclose three small tarns.

Accommodation in the vicinity is limited to one first-class hotel with sporting facilities and smaller establishments offering bed and breakfast, a youth hostel, and a camping site in Grizedale Forest. *Early closing—Thursdays, winter only; Limited bus service; Nearest station—Windermere via the ferry.*

KENDAL (pop. 21,830) Lying in the valley of the River Kent, the town's grey-limestone houses are flanked on either side by steep fells, with the mountains of Lakeland forming an impressive backcloth. Kendal has a long and stormy history including violent and bloody Scots raids, against which the narrow cobbled yards or courts are said to have been built as a system of defence. In 1331, Flemish weavers settled here and for 600 years the woollen industry flourished—the town's motto being 'Wool is my Bread.' As the industry declined, others took its place, namely shoe, snuff and tobacco-manufacturing and engineering works. Kendal mint cake can be bought at many of the excellent shops as well as items made locally from horn. The Norman **castle,** though now in ruins, was built by Ivo de Tallebois in 1085. This was the birthplace of Queen Katherine Parr in 1512, the sixth wife of Henry VIII—who survived him. There is free access to the castle which affords fine views. The **Church of the Holy Trinity** in Kirkland dates from the 13th century and is one of the largest parish churches in England, having five wide aisles. Of interest are the colours of the 55th Westmorland Regiment: the Parr, Bellingham and Strickland chapels; and some fine memorials and brasses. Nearby, **Abbot Hall Art Gallery,** built in 1759 and recently restored to 18th-century decor, contains period furniture, china, glass and silver in addition to a collection of paintings by artists including Romney and Turner. There are four galleries on the first floor where craft exhibitions are staged. Open daily 10.30 am– 5.30 pm, except Saturday and Sunday when it opens from 2–5 pm.

The **Museum of Lakeland Life and Industry,** opening times as above, stands adjacent to Abbot Hall and displays farm implements and equipment used by local craftsmen, including wheelwrights, blacksmiths and bobbin-makers over 100 years ago. A fully-furnished Lakeland parlour at the turn of the century, and above it a similar bedroom, are of special note. Children will enjoy a collection of Arthur Ransome's *Swallows and Amazons* books, together with furniture and personal items on show in the library (by special appointment). The museum recently acquired the the **Old Grammar School,** for a museum specializing in early toys and games.

The **Brewery Arts and Community Centre** in Highgate, as its name suggests, is a community centre for the arts and sciences housed in a converted brewery. Open daily 11 am–11 pm, it offers a wide range of educational and craft activities, folk, rock and jazz concerts, live theatre, ballet, music and lectures. Catering facilities are available. Also in Highgate, the **Town Hall,** though a fairly modern building, has much of interest. The tall clock tower has a unique carillon which plays English, Irish, Scottish and Welsh airs daily. The Mayor's Parlour contains paintings by Romney and Queen Katherine Parr's Book of Devotions. In front of the Town Hall stands the ancient **Call Stone,** the base of the market cross, where successive English monarchs have been proclaimed for many hundreds of years.

The **Borough Museum** in Station Road houses comprehensive geological and natural history sections, a collection of big game specimens being particularly impressive. Open 10 am–4.30 pm weekdays. An interesting Tudor house, **Castle Dairy** in Wildman Street, is open on weekdays from 2–4 pm. There is a unique Clavey mantlepiece in the dining room, and in the bedroom upstairs a great four-poster bed and rare ambrey.

Away from the town's busy streets are many quiet parks and open spaces where visitors can enjoy peaceful surroundings. An additional attraction in August is the Kendal Gathering comprising two weeks of exhibitions, plays, sports meetings and other events.

The A6, A684 and A685 converge on the town with access points to the M6 motorway approximately 7 km (4 ml) to the east, and the western by-pass road affords a through link to the Lake District. For sportsmen there is good angling in the local rivers, an 18-hole golf course and public swimming baths in Allhallows Lane.

There are many hotels and guesthouses of all categories within the town, local inns and farmhouses provide bed and breakfast, and there are a number of caravan sites nearby. *Early closing—Thursday; Market day— Saturday; Public Transport— Ribble Motor Services, Kendal Bus Station, Blackhall Road. Tel. (0539) 20932; By rail—Oxenholme Station on the outskirts of the town provides main line connections north and south, and Kendal Station is on the branch line from Oxenholme to Windermere; Tourist and Information Office—Town Hall, Highgate. Tel. (0539) 23649 Ext. 53.*
KESWICK (pop. 4500) Dominated by the Skiddaw range, the town stands at the head of Derwent Water, and good road links provided by way of the A66, A591 and B5289 make this a popular touring centre (see Tours 6, 7, 8, 9, 10). Steamers sail the lake from Good Friday to mid-October, and boats can be hired from Keswick, Portinscale and Lodore. The Fitz Park Trust Art Gallery and Museum, the Pencil Museum and the Model Railway Exhibition offer something of interest to suit most tastes. Within walking distance are **Lingholm Gardens,** Portinscale, Crosthwaite Church and **Castlerigg Stone Circle,** with fine viewpoints from Castlerigg and Latrigg. Sporting facilities include sailing, pony trekking and fishing. The mobile Century Theatre is based at Keswick during the summer, and offers productions with a modern approach.

There is the widest possible range of accommodation from large hotels to small guesthouses, self-catering flats and cottages, and sites for both static and touring caravans and tents. *Early closing— Wednesday (not during the season); Market day—Saturday, also Wednesday (June to November); The Cumberland Bus Company run day and half-day excursions, booking at The Bus Station, Tithebarn Street. Tel. (0596) 72791. Davies of Keswick run mini-bus excursions daily, details from 23 Helvellyn Street. Tel. (0596) 72676; Nearest Station— Penrith, with connecting bus services; Information Offices—Main Street. Tel. (0596) 72645; and from Easter to the end of October, The Moot Hall, Market Square. Tel. (0596) 72645.*
KIRKOSWALD (pop. 655) A village of great interest situated by the Raven Beck and on the B6413. The church, built over the site of an ancient Saxon well, contains much medieval work. It was

founded by St Aidan and is
dedicated to King, later Saint
Oswald. An unusual feature, the
separate church tower, stands
further up the hill. Across the road,
the college was founded for six
priests in the 16th century. The
house contains fine panelling,
period furniture and an interesting
display of weapons. Open by
written appointment only with the
owner Mr T. R. Fetherstonhaugh.
The 14th-century castle, built on
high ground, is now a ruin, but the
moat can still be traced and
evidence of vaulted dungeons,
towers and the gatehouse can be
seen. There is free access across a
field.
On an unclassified road 2½ km
(1½ ml) to the north west are

Nunnery Walks at Staffield. A
path leaves the car-park at
Armathwaite Nunnery and crosses
the fields before reaching the River
Eden and the confluence with the
Croglin Beck. The tour follows the
river past a series of waterfalls
before returning to the car-park.

There is excellent local fishing,
but accommodation in Kirkoswald
for fishermen and visitors is
extremely limited. *Local bus
services operated by the Ribble
Motor Services connect the village
to Penrith and Carlisle; Nearest
town and station—Penrith.*
LEVENS (pop. 895) Lies 6½ km
(4 ml) south of Kendal off the A6.
The rural setting, on raised ground
with views across the Lyth Valley
to the white cliffs of Whitbarrow

Levens Hall

Scar once the coastline of Morecambe Bay, produces a peaceful atmosphere so near to the bustle of holiday traffic. Two of the greatest houses of Cumbria, Sizergh Castle and Levens Park, are situated near the village.

Sizergh Castle (National Trust) has been the home of the Strickland family for over 700 years. The pele tower was built in 1340 and forms the basis for the present house, which is mostly 16th century, containing a wealth of oak panelling, especially in the great hall. Sizergh is also renowned for its five carved overmantles, wood-ribbed or plaster ceilings and adze-hewn oak floors. The walls are hung with paintings by Romney, Kneller and others, together with examples of Flemish tapestry and an extensive collection of Tudor and Jacobean furniture. Open from the end of April to September on Wednesdays, the gardens are also open on Tuesday and Thursday, 2–5.45 pm. Parties are accepted at other times by prior arrangement with Mrs Hornyold-Strickland at the castle.

A short distance to the south east at the junction of the A6 and A590 stands **Levens Hall,** the greatest Elizabethan house in Cumbria, with famous topiary gardens laid out in 1700 during the reign of James II. The first hall was probably built in the 13th century, all that remains of that period is the pele tower which now forms part of the 16th-century building. The beautiful panelling was added about 1580, as were the richly carved plasterwork ceilings. Of particular interest is the Charles II furniture, fine silver and paintings by Lely, Cuyp and Rubens. The house and the steam-engine collection, part of which is housed in the Old Brew House, are open from May 1st–17th September, on Tuesday, Wednesday, Thursday and Sunday from 2–5 pm; also on Spring and Summer Bank Holidays. The gardens are open daily from 10 am–5 pm. Visitors are requested not to bring dogs. There is a free car-park and tea room. From the hall, the visitors have a choice of routes; the A590 continues to Grange-over-Sands, passing beneath the towering limestone cliffs, once the coastline before the sea slowly receded during the centuries, then on to the coast; while the A5074 leads to Windermere town and the lake. Looking to the south, before the road divides, notice the unusual round chimneys of 16th-century **Nether Levens Hall.**

LORTON (pop. 235) The two villages of High and Low Lorton lie in the valley of the River Cocker beyond the northern reaches of Crummock Water (see Tours 8 and 10). At **Lorton Hall,** the present pele tower dates from the 15th century, and is incorporated into a later range of domestic buildings (see page 16). The villages mark one of the resting places of St Cuthbert, and the church is dedicated to the saint. Lorton is within easy reach of Cockermouth and Keswick, respectively north and east on the B5292. Sailing is possible on Crummock Water, Loweswater and Buttermere (no powerboats). Application should be made to the National Trust, which also owns the fishing rights. The Melbreak Hunt meet regularly in the area. *Nearest Station—Penrith.*

MILLOM (pop. 7055) Stands on the most southerly tip of the Copeland district on the A5093 and A595 (Tour 4). The ruined castle and Holy Trinity Old Church lie to the north of the town watched over by Black Combe. Of interest to visitors is the recently opened Folk Museum described on page 23. The extensive sandy beaches continue to the village of Haverigg, where there are various holiday amenities, especially good for children.

Accommodation is limited to smaller establishments, self-catering cottages and chalets, caravan and camping sites. The Millom Show, which attracts large crowds, is held on the last Saturday in August. *Early closing— Wednesday; On major bus routes; On British Rail branch line from Whitehaven and Barrow; Tourist Information Centre—The Folk Museum, St George's Road. Tel. (0657) 2555.*

MORESBY (pop. 1120) A small, scattered village by the Cumbrian coast situated between Workington and Whitehaven. The small 19th-century church has been built on the cliffs overlooking the Irish Sea. From the churchyard, a path leads to the beach past the remains of a Roman coastal station dating from AD 130. A short distance inland across the A595, is the intimate theatre of **Rosehill,** set in the grounds of Sir Nicholas Seker's gracious 18th-century mansion. Details are given on page 36. A restaurant is attached to the theatre with facilities for late-night dining.

Accommodation in the area is very limited and visitors should apply to either Whitehaven or Workington Information Centres for advice. *Bus services are provided by the Cumberland Motor Services Ltd; Nearest main-line station—Whitehaven.*

NEWBY BRIDGE Situated on the A590, one of the main arteries of Lakeland, and the A592 from Windermere and Bowness, has an unusual stone bridge of five unequal arches marking the end of navigable water on the River Leven, at the foot of Windermere. The surrounding fields dip gently towards the water providing a pleasing setting for the scattered houses. Although accommodation is limited, this makes an excellent centre for touring the Furness Fells and Grizedale Forest, where a circular tour could include the Georgian **Rusland Hall,** its gardens together with the gardens of **Graythwaite Hall,** peaceful Cartmel Fell and, further south west, the sandy beaches of Morecambe Bay. Nearer at hand, at Backbarrow, where the river rushes over a series of weirs and rapids on its way to the sea, can be found the old charcoal-burning iron foundry, only recently closed down. Although not open to the public, parts of the bloomeries (charcoal-burning iron furnaces) can be seen. From Haverthwaite, the Railway Society operates services for Lakeside connecting with the Sealink steamers; combined tickets are available.

Hotels in the area provide amenities for shooting, golf and tennis in addition to watersports of all kinds. At **Fell Foot,** the National Trust have chalets and a touring-caravan park. *Ribble Motor Service buses serve the area: Nearest station—Windermere.*

PENRITH (pop. 10,945) Served by many roads and only 8 km (5 ml) from Ullswater, this interesting old town makes an excellent touring centre. The A6, A66, A686 and B5288 converge on the town, which is skirted on the west by the M6 motorway. Reminders of the dark days of the border raids are evident in the narrow streets which retain the names of Burrowgate, Castlegate, Friarsgate, Middlegate and Southgate, and the entrances and courtyards where cattle were driven for safety during the fierce fighting. The **castle,** originally built in 1397, was substantially enlarged in 1483 by Richard, Duke of Gloucester, who was to become Richard III. However, by 1550, it was virtually a ruin, large quantities of stone having been removed. In 1913, the castle was handed to the Commission for the Protection of Ancient Monuments and Historic Buildings, which excavated the site and made safe the stonework. The surrounding land has now been developed into an attractive park, a pleasant feature of the town. **St Andrew's Church** combines Norman and Georgian architecture. On the north-west corner of the tower, is an ornament bearing the arms of the Earls of Warwick who were closely connected with the town during the 14th and 15th centuries. Two interesting stone effigies of Anthony Hutton and his wife stand on the steps of the three-sided gallery. The east window contains beautiful stained glass, and windows on the north and south side of the church show portraits of Richard II or III and Richard, Duke of York. In the churchyard are interesting stones, one, the Giant's Grave, is said to be that of Owain, King of Cumbria from 920–37, whilst the other smaller stone, the Giant's Thumb, is thought to have been erected by him as a memorial. Also in the churchyard is the 16th-century building, formerly the grammar school. Nearby, a red-sandstone Tudor house, now a restaurant, was at one time **Dame Birkett's**

School attended by Wordsworth, his sister Dorothy and his future wife Mary. Two of the town's hotels were originally mansions; the present **Gloucester Arms** is thought to have been the home of Richard III, his coat of arms can be seen over the entrance, and the interior has some fine old oak panelling; the **Two Lions Hotel** belonged to Gerald Lowther and has a unique plasterwork ceiling. **Hutton Hall** in Friargate, dated 1480, includes a pele tower and was the home of the Hutton family. Here the Duke of Cumberland was entertained after the battle at Clifton Moor. The house is now owned by the Penrith Masonic Hall Co. Ltd.

Penrith Beacon, 285 m (937 ft), stands above the town and is easily reached by footpath. From the summit there are excellent views of the surrounding countryside and distant peaks of Lakeland. The beacon was lit as a warning in times of trouble for hundreds of years, notably in 1745 as warning of the Jacobite Rising, and finally in 1804 during the Napoleonic Wars.

The lakes and mountains of the Lake District National Park are within easy reach to the west (Tour 7 ii).

Just north of the town lies **Hutton-in-the-Forest,** home of Lord Inglewood. The mansion stands between two pele towers and contains exquisite carvings, tapestries and period furniture. Open by appointment only. Contact the Head Gardener. Tel. Skelton 265.

An interesting tour from Penrith is by way of the A686 and B6412 through the Eden Valley to Great Salkeld, Kirkoswald and Nunnery Walks.

Leisure activities include angling,

sailing on Ullswater (buses from
Penrith connect with the lake
steamers at Pooley Bridge), an
18-hole golf course and local pony
trekking. The Ullswater Fell Pack
hunt regularly in the area.

There is a wide range of
accommodation including large
hotels, guesthouses, self-catering
holidays, camping sites and youth
hostels. *Early closing—Wednesday;
Market days—Tuesday and
Saturday; Local bus services
operated by Ribble Motor Services,
which also organizes day and half-
day excursions. Further details
from the offices in Middlegate.
Tel. (0768) 3616; Information
centres—Town Clerk's Department,
Town Hall; The Public Library; or
Robinson's School, Middlegate.
Tel. (0768) 2201.*

RAVENGLASS A small village of
one main street situated on the
estuary of the River Esk, which was
once an important Roman trading
port. Nearby, the unique **Walls
Castle,** the villa of a local
commander is well worth visiting,
although necessitating a short
walk. 'La'al Ratty' the narrow-
guage railway, runs from the
village to Dalegarth through
delightful countryside and is a
must for all visitors. **Muncaster
Castle** the home of Sir Ramsden-
Pennington, Bart., is described on
page 59 and is passed on the
unclassified road leading to
Hardknott and Wrynose Passes.
An excellent centre for
ornithologists at the **Drigg Dunes
Nature Reserve** and Gullery
presents opportunities to observe
the greater black-backed gulls;
while the mudflats are a haven for
all types of waders (see also page
89). Boats are available for day sea
fishing and enquiries should be
made at the inn.

Accommodation is very limited
in the area, but the village is
accessible from all the coast towns
on the A595 coast road. *Local
transport—the Cumberland Motor
Service; British Rail branch line
from Barrow-in-Furness to
Workington.*

RYDAL (pop. 345) This small
village stands at the foot of Rydal
Water, surrounded by steep fells.
Only two miles from Ambleside, the
A591 passes through the village
(Tour 6). Rydal Mount, where
Wordsworth lived from 1813 until
his death in 1850, stands on a
hillside above the lake. The village
is within walking distance of the
lakes of Grasmere and Windermere,
and a short car ride to Keswick
and Bowness. The Vale of Rydal
Sheepdog Trials held annually at
Rydal Hall are a popular
attraction (see page 34). Sporting
facilities include sailing and
boating on Grasmere and
Windermere, fishing in Rydal
Water and local lakes and rivers,
mountaineering—the Langdales,
Scafell, Great Gable and Pillar are
within easy reach—and local pony
trekking. A National Trust Nature
Trail runs from **White Moss** along
the shore of the lake.

There is excellent accommodation
of every kind within the immediate
vicinity. *Local bus service
provided by Ribble Motor Service
Ltd; Nearest Station—Windermere.*

SEASCALE (pop. 2106) A seaside
resort with long sandy beaches, yet
only 19 km (12 ml) from Wast
Water. The town's main road is the
B5344, which joins the A595 at
Gosforth. The church of St
Cuthbert, consecrated in 1890,
contains interesting wood carvings.

Nearby on the A595 stands
Calder Bridge, and beyond, the
impressive ruins of the Cistercian

abbey. To the side of the abbey, the mansion house has a Georgian façade, added in the 18th century. Now in private ownership, view from the road. To the south west of Calder Bridge, and in stark contrast, is Calder Hall Atomic Power Station.

Seascale has much to offer the sportsman. The sailing club has launching facilities for small craft. There is an 18-hole golf course, and for fishermen good sea and river angling. There are nature reserves at Ravenglass and St Bees of interest to ornithologists (see page 31).

Hotel accommodation is available within the town. *Early closing— Thursday; Bus services provided by Cumberland Motor Services; Nearest Station—Sellafield for Whitehaven and Carlisle.*

SHAP (pop. 1180) A small village near Shap summit with extensive views towards Lakeland mountain ranges. In winter, roads in the area can prove hazardous, including the M6 motorway and the parallel A6. Of historical interest is the great **Shap Abbey;** hidden from sight in the Lowther Valley and surrounded by woodland are the remains of this monastic building founded at the end of the 12th century for monks of the Premonstratensian Order. The ruins seen today are mainly of the 15th century, only the striking west tower, reaching almost to full height, showing the glories of the past. In the care of the Department of the Environment it is open at standard times. A short distance away is the tiny 16th-century pre-Reformation chapel of Keld (National Trust). To obtain the key (available at all reasonable times) see a notice on the chapel door.

A lane leading north westwards from the abbey passes the **Thunder Stone,** a large boulder which marks the end of an avenue of standing stones over 1 km ($\frac{3}{4}$ ml) long leading from a massive $24\frac{1}{2}$ m- (80 ft) diameter stone circle which was partly destroyed in the building of the railway. Continue on to Bampton for the beautiful Hawswater Reservoir, Askham and Lowther Park (Tour 7 ii). Unclassified roads lead eastwards across gently rolling lower fells to the attractive towns of Crosby Ravensworth and Appleby.

Limited hotel, guesthouse and farm accommodation is available in the area. *Early closing— Thursday and Saturday; Market day—Monday; National Buses stop in the village by request; The railway station is on the main line to London and Glasgow.*

ST BEES (pop. 1245) A small seaside village on the B5345 and a short detour from the A595 which passes through Calder Bridge, Egremont and Whitehaven. Legend tells us that it was here St Bega, an Irish Princess, founded a nunnery in AD 650, and it was from her that the village derived its name. The nunnery was destroyed during the Viking invasion and a new foundation created by William de Meschines in 1120. The red-sandstone building contains many fine examples of Norman workmanship including the famous Dragon Stone to be seen in the wall opposite the west door. Remains of priory buildings can be traced to the south of the church (which remains in constant use). Across the road is St Bees school, founded in 1583 at the bequest of Edmund Grindal, Archbishop of York and Canterbury, who was born locally. There are some old houses in Main Street, notably Stone House Farm, next to the car-park, where two stones bear the dates of 1660 and 1712. From the car-park there is a pleasant walk on to Tomlin Head and Fleswick Bay, a small cove with a polished pebble beach. Further along the cliff is the lighthouse where it is possible, at times, to be shown round. The headland is also an RSPB Nature Reserve which may be viewed from the path, permits are not required. There is no access to the reserve for vehicular traffic either from St Bees or Sandwith. The pleasant sandy beach beneath the red-sandstone cliffs is safe for bathing at low tide (not off the rocks), and can be reached from the short promenade. Visitors are welcome at St Bees school nine-hole golf course, and tennis and pony trekking are available in the area. The town makes an excellent centre for Eskdale and Ennerdale with facilities for climbing in the Great Gable and Scafell ranges.

Limited accommodation is available in hotels and guesthouses. A large camping site facing the beach has facilities for touring caravans and tents and provides excellent amenities. *Cumberland Motor Services buses call in the village; The railway station is on the Whitehaven to Barrow and Carlisle line.*

TROUTBECK (pop. 345) A tiny hillside village lying on the A592 Windermere to Penrith road at the foot of the Kirkstone Pass. The wayside church, built in 1736 and refurnished in 1861, stands on the site of an earlier chapel. The royal arms of George II are above the door, there is interesting 17th-century woodcarving and a beautiful east window by Edward Burne-Jones, William Morris and Ford Maddox-Brown.

On an unclassified road south of the village, **Townend** is an excellent example of a 17th-century manor house. Many generations of the Browne family lived here until 1943, and in 1947 the house came into the care of the National Trust. The living-room and bedrooms contain period furniture, pottery and glassware, and there is an extensive collection of books in the library. Open on Wednesday all the year round from 2–6 pm; Easter–September daily, except Saturday and Monday.

Troutbeck stands in magnificent mountaineering country, with winter skiing nearby on the Kirkstone Pass; all watersports are catered for on Windermere and there is local pony trekking. *A very limited bus service operates; Nearest town and station—Windermere.*

ULLSWATER The villages of Patterdale, Glenridding, Pooley Bridge and Howtown are grouped round the shores of Ullswater, a large lake with three distinct reaches (see Tour 7). A steamer plys the lake during the summer; boats are available for hire and it is possible to launch private dinghies. Patterdale has connections with St Patrick, a church and holy well dedicated to the saint will be found in the village. Glenridding, Pooley Bridge and Howtown are all stopping points for the steamer. The waterfalls at **Aira Force** are a popular attraction.

Sporting facilities include pony trekking, sailing and fishing, with mountaineering and rock climbing on nearby fells. The Ullswater Pack meet regularly in the area. Sheep dog trials are held on the last Saturday in August.

There is a wide range of accommodation available, together with caravan and camping sites.

Local bus services connect all the villages with Penrith, and are provided by Ribble Motor Services Ltd; Nearest Station—Penrith; Information Office—Lake District National Park Mobile Unit, Beck Side Car-Park, Glenridding.

ULVERSTON (pop. 12,300) A pleasant market town backed by the Southern Lakeland fells which has been the centre of Furness since early Roman times. Now a blend of the old and the new, with old quays and narrow alleys. Parts of the town are 12th century, for example, the foundation of the 19th-century church of St Mary, where the market charter of 1280 is kept. Modern Ulverston, birthplace of Stan Laurel, includes a covered market and the fine Coronation Hall where music and drama productions are staged, dances and exhibitions held. A notable landmark on Hoad Hill is the monument erected in memory of Sir John Barrow, author and Arctic explorer.

On the southern outskirts of the town stands **Swarthmoor Hall,** an Elizabethan house with mullioned windows, a fine oak staircase and many panelled rooms. Built by Judge Fell in 1688, it became the home of George Fox, founder of the Quaker movement when he married Margaret, the widow of Judge Fell. On the shore of Morecambe Bay, **Connishead Priory** overlooks Chapel Island on which are the remains of a small oratory where prayers were said for travellers crossing the dangerous sands.

The town makes an excellent centre from which to tour the interesting Furness Peninsula villages of Pennington with the nearby barrows known as **'Ella'** and **'Conynger'** and ancient church; the Neolithic circles on **Birkrigg Common**; the **Urswick** stone walls, remains of a pre-Roman settlement and church founded in AD 877. At Aldingham, a visit should be made to St Cuthbert's Church associated with Lady Jane Gray. The long stretches of sandy beach from Bardsea to Rampside are safe for children and swimming at high tide, although there is a pool in the town for inclement weather. From here, Tour 1 may be joined at Newby Bridge and Tours 3 and 4 via the A595 at Broughton-in-Furness. Visits can also be made to Dalton and Barrow on the A590, A5087 and A595, not forgetting **Furness Abbey.** *Early closing—Wednesday; Market day—Thursday; The area is served by the Cumberland Motor Services and Ribble; It is on the British Rail main line to Barrow.*

WHITEHAVEN (pop. 25,955) Has developed from a small fishing village in the estates of Sir Christopher Lowther into a port of considerable size. Served by the A595 coast road from Dalton-in-Furness, 72½ km (45 ml), to Carlisle, approximately 63 km (39 ml), it is within easy reach of Northern Lakeland. The interesting docks now cater for a growing fishing industry and a thriving import/export trade of coal, chemicals and timber. The south harbour has been converted to a fine pleasure yachting anchorage. Of great interest to American visitors, the churchyard of St Nicholas contains the grave of George Washington's grandmother; other associations with the family are to be found at Helton Flechan, near the county's eastern boundary and at Warton, near Carnforth, Lancashire

South of the industrial town of Distington will be found the site of

Heys Castle with one wall
standing. At **Moresby,** Sir Oliver
Messel has created a delightful
theatre in the grounds of Sir
Nicholas Seker's 18th-century
mansion. Details are on page 36
Within easy reach are the
interesting castle town of
Egremont and St Bees with its fine
Norman abbey.

Within the town, the Civic Hall
provides regular music and drama
programmes and stages the annual
Music Festival. The new sports
hall caters for all types of sport and
has all the latest equipment.
Whitehaven provides excellent
fishing for visitors from the rivers
of the Esk, Duddon and Calder,
and the lakes of Devoke Water,
Ennerdale and Wast Water. Deep-
sea fishing is also available.
Visitors may obtain further
information from the centre in the
Civic Hall. The coastline affords
excellent and safe swimming, but
pools in the town and at Egremont
cater for inclement weather.

Accommodation is rather limited.
*Early closing—Wednesday; Market
days—Thursday and Saturday;
Transport is provided by the
Cumberland Motor Services buses;
On the British Rail line from
Carlisle; Information Centre—
Civic Hall, Lowther Street. Tel.
(0946) 2778.*
WIGTON (pop. 4880) Situated in
the fertile plain between the
Solway Firth and the Skiddaw
Forest, Wigton, known locally as
the 'throstle's nest', is the main
market town for a wide area. There
are excellent road links to Carlisle;
Cockermouth and the coast;
Keswick and Northern Lakeland,
provided by the A596, B5305
connecting with the A595, B5302
and B5303. The red-sandstone parish
church is dedicated to St Mary,

and a memorial fountain
commemorates the wife of George
Moore. Charles Dickens and
Wilkie Collins visited the town,
Dickens later writing *The Lazy
Tour of Two Idle Apprentices.*
Mentioned in the book are the old
parish pump and a tall gaslamp;
both can still be seen in the park.
Sports facilities include local
fishing and an indoor swimming
pool. A market charter was granted
in 1262 by Henry III, and livestock
markets are held weekly on
Tuesdays. An annual sale of 500
horses on the third or fourth
Wednesday in October attracts
buyers from many parts of the
country.

There is a wide range of
accommodation available. *Market
day—Tuesday; Cumberland Bus
Services operate from Whitehaven
in the west to Carlisle in the east;
Wigton Station is on the Carlisle to
Whitehaven line.*
WINDERMERE AND BOWNESS
(pop. 7860) Are well placed to cater
for the holidaymaker. Their
position is on the east shore of the
lake at the busy confluence of
Lakeland's main arteries; the
A5074 and the A6 which passes
through the delightful Lyth Valley
and joins the A592 which follows
the shore from Newby Bridge. From
Kendal, the A591 passes through
attractive, rolling hills before
dropping down into the town centre
then continuing northwards to
Ambleside and the heart of
Lakeland.

All kinds of sport are catered for
in the area, either for the
individual or in one of the
residential centres (see Activity
Holidays page 40). Watersports
predominate, sailing being the most
popular. During the season the
lake will seem alive with every type

of craft, the colourful sails and spinnakers billowing in the gentle breezes. Water skiers enjoy the long stretch of water, and power boat enthusiasts have their own Record Week in October. Sealink cruisers ply between Waterhead, Ambleside; Bowness and Lakeside, connecting with the Steam Railway from Haverthwaite; combined tickets are available. Belle Isle can be visited by a regular service operating from Cockshott Point. Many gentle walks can be taken through the parks and guided walks are arranged from Bowness Bay Information Centre to all the beauty spots. Tuition and facilities are also available for golf (18-hole course), climbing, walking, angling, grass skiing, archery, canoeing and pony trekking.

First-class accommodation is available—four hotels having private swimming pools—to smaller establishments, self-catering flats and apartments, a youth hostel and numerous caravan and camping sites. The main season is from Easter to the end of September, although some hotels remain open all the year. Bicycles, self-drive cars, taxis and coaches are available for hire locally. *Early closing—Thursday (although many shops stay open during the season); The towns are served by the Ribble and Cumberland Bus Services, also the National Express Service from all parts of the country; The Mountain Goat mini-bus service operates throughout Lakeland and information can be obtained from Elleray Garage, Victoria Street, Windermere; Windermere Station is the terminus of the branch line from Oxenholme where connections can be made to London, Euston and Glasgow; Information Centres—The Lake District National Park Centre, The Glebe, provides information on the park, films and exhibitions. Tel. (096 62) 2895; also at Brockhole where there is an interpretive centre. Tel. (096 62) 2231 and Bank House, High Street; South Lakeland Tourism and Recreational Centre, Ashleigh, Windermere.*

WORKINGTON (pop. 28,700) An important industrial town situated on the Solway coast at the mouth of the River Derwent. The A596, A597 and A595 provide good road links to all parts of Lakeland. The history of the town is interwoven with the Curwen family who built Workington Hall, now in a poor state of repair and not open to the public. The Helena Thompson Museum contains Victorian objects of interest and costumes displayed in period room settings. Open Tuesday to Saturday, 10 am– 12 noon and 2–4.30 pm. The busy docks and harbour have much to interest the visitor, with both coasting and foreign-going vessels to be seen.

Many of the northern lakes are within easy reach, notably Bassenthwaite, Ennerdale, Loweswater, Crummock Water and Buttermere. Sports facilities include an 18-hole golf course, a competition swimming pool at the Moorclose Sports Centre and fishing in local lakes and rivers. Sailors can use the slipway of the sailing club to launch private dinghies.

Accommodation within the town is extremely limited. *Early closing— Thursday; Market day— Wednesday; Bus services are provided by the Cumberland Motor Services Ltd; Rail connections from Workington Station to Barrow or Carlisle for the main London to Carlisle line.*

INDEX

All places which have a main entry, and the pages on which these occur, are printed in heavy type. Asterisks indicate illustrations. Map references are printed last in italic.